WALKS THROUGH HISTORY

EXPLORING THE
EAST END

WALKS THROUGH HISTORY

EXPLORING THE EAST END

ROSEMARY TAYLOR

breedon **books**
PUBLISHING

First published in Great Britain in 2001 by
The Breedon Books Publishing Company Limited
Breedon House, 3 The Parker Centre, Derby, DE21 4SZ.

Reprinted 2004

Acknowledgements

Pictures on pages 6 and 8 courtesy of Joan Vicente.
Pictures on pages 27 and 101 courtesy of Philip Mexnick.
Pictures on pages 16, 21, 29, 61, 63, 70, 77, 79, 84, 92, 106, 119, 121, 126, 127, 131,
133, 138, 142 and 166 courtesy of Tower Hamlets Local History Library and Archives.
All other pictures are from the author's own collection.

ISBN 1 85983 270 9

Printed and bound by Scotprint

Contents

Frederick John Phillips, who worked all his life for Mann Crossman and Paulin Brewers, in Stepney Green with his bicycle, 1897.

Introduction

The London Borough of Tower Hamlets, familiarly known as the East End of London, or simply the East End, has a rich, complex history going back to the Domesday Book, where it is recorded as Stebunhithe, the Manor of Stepney, belonging to the Bishop of London. The name Tower Hamlets is itself evocative, for it is indeed a group of 21 hamlets by the Tower of London, bordered by the City gates of Aldgate and Bishopsgate on its western extreme and the River Lea on the east, while to the north, Victoria Park's northern perimeter forms a natural demarcation, and the River Thames flows to the south.

The East End has played a significant role in the history of London, yet has retained its own unique identity through centuries of change. A thousand years of history have taken the ancient parish of Stepney, once an idyllic rural retreat from the grimy, smoky city of London, where gentle folk came to breathe the fresh country air, through a gradual expansion, as the building of the docks and the proliferation of factories and industries served to create a vast slum of seething humanity, interspersed with gracious mansions and elegant town houses. One hundred years ago, a population explosion necessitated a re-drawing of the boundaries, and the area was carved up into the three Metropolitan Boroughs of Stepney, Bethnal Green and Poplar. Sixty-five years later, the three boroughs were merged to form the London Borough of Tower Hamlets. However, the communities have clung stubbornly to their own identities, and nowhere else in London is the old village name used as a matter of course. Eastenders will tell you they come from Stepney, Bow, Limehouse, Wapping, Poplar, Whitechapel, Bromley-by-Bow, Blackwall, Bethnal Green or Mile End, rarely from Tower Hamlets.

Communities as diverse as the Huguenots, Germans, Irish, Russian and Polish Jews, Chinese and more recently Bangladeshis have left their mark upon the common heritage. Two World Wars have significantly altered the landscape, indeed the Blitz almost succeeded in wiping the East End off the map. But, while so many landmarks disappeared, new ones have taken their place. The docks, once the hub of the British Empire, now serve as London's new financial and business heart, with Canary Wharf a prominent symbol of new wealth and influence. However, through all these changes, it is still possible to travel through time, following the trails of famous and infamous characters, communities and events, some of national and international significance, to explore the rich history and cultural diversity to be found in the highways, back streets and alleys of the East End.

This selection of illustrated guided tours of the East End is the result of several years' research. Each trail is meticulously planned in a circular route, and almost all of them begin and end at an underground station. Alternatively, enjoy travelling around the East End of London from the comfort of your armchair. Each stopping point along the selected route is marked on the map, its historical significance is detailed, and illustrations highlight interesting and unusual features of both past and present.

Walk 1
Wapping and the Highway

When journeying eastwards from London, at the Tower of London the traveller enters Wapping, the first riverside hamlet of the East End. The name itself dates from the fifth century, and Wapping was then a marsh on the riverbank, east of Londinium, the ancient British village which the Romans had developed. The Roman wall on the east of the town ran through the present site of the Tower of London, and excavations have uncovered sections of it, which can be seen near Tower Hill station. Archaeologists have also found the remains of a Roman road near the Highway, which led to a watchtower at Shadwell.

From London three main roads ran eastwards. The main thoroughfare was Ratcliff Highway, now known simply as the Highway, which continued along through Limehouse to Poplar. A second road, running close to the river, was known as Wapping High Street and Wapping Wall, and came up to meet the Highway at Shadwell. Further to the north was Cable Street, part of which was known as Knockfergus and inhabited by Irish settlers. The main north to south route was Old Gravel Lane, now Wapping Lane. The first Anglo-Saxons probably built their settlement here on the gravel above the marsh and the name Wapping probably derived from a chieftain, Waeppa, and means 'the people of Waeppa'. The gravel starts at the Highway and goes down toward the river at Shadwell, finally reaching the shore at Ratcliffe Cross.

By the 15th century wharves, warehouses and docks had been constructed all along the north bank of the Thames. The first dock was at St Katharine's, with others at Wapping, Shadwell and Ratcliff. Wapping Dock was just large enough to allow small craft to tie up, with wooden stairs leading to the water. As was customary up to the end of the 18th century, larger ships moored out in the river, and cargo and passengers were brought ashore by boats or lighters.

During Henry VIII's reign an Act of Parliament was passed, in 1535–6, to engage the services of a Dutchman, Cornelius Vanderdelft, to drain the marshes of Wapping. Vanderdelft's drainage scheme was successful and the development of Wapping from the Tower to Shadwell was then assured.

The chapel of St John the Evangelist was consecrated in 1617 as a chapel of ease for Wapping. By 1694 Wapping St John had become a parish in its own right. The church was rebuilt in 1760, but the destruction of World War Two has left only the church tower standing, while the school beside it has been converted into apartments.

St Paul's at Shadwell became a parish church in 1670, and New Gravel Lane and parts of Wapping to the east, including Wapping Wall, formed part of the new parish.

John Rocque's Map of London of 1746 depicts all the streets of Wapping, and Nightingale Lane, Old Gravel Lane, New Gravel Lane, Great Hermitage Street, and Anchor and Hope Alley are all shown, along with Love Lane and Labour-in-Vain Street. Upper and Lower Wapping were orchards and gardens planted to drain the marsh and draw moisture from the soil. The London Docks, in the building of which a large number of houses and streets were demolished, covered

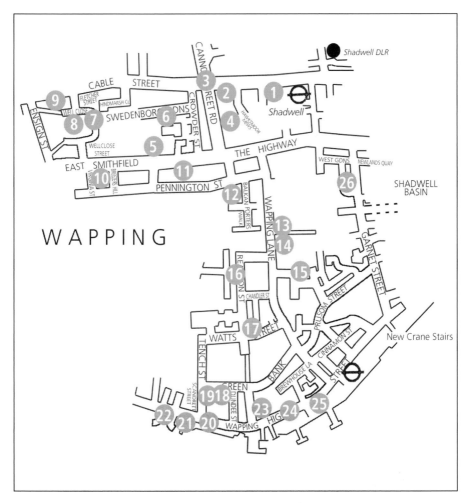

this area. However, between Rosemary Lane and East Smithfield there were the less salubrious places, such as Harebrain Court, Money Bag Alley, Cherubim Court, Hog Yard, Black Jack, Black Dog and Black Boy Alleys, and dozens more. In these alleys lived workmen and tradesmen of every description. There were stevedores, watermen, ship's bakers, marine store dealers, suppliers of rope and tackle, instrument makers and boat builders, carpenters and smiths. There were also lodging houses, brothels and pawnshops, and public houses and taverns. All these places have now disappeared, to be replaced by large blocks of 19th-century flats.

In 1723, Nicholas Hawksmoor completed his magnificent church St George-in-the-East, built on the brow of the red cliff that gives its name to Ratcliff. It became a new parish church for Wapping Stepney.

Prior to the building of the East and West India Docks, all merchandise had to pass through

St George-in-the-East Church, viewed from Tobacco Dock, Wapping.

Ratcliffe Murders. Three members of the Marr family and their shop boy were brutally murdered, then 12 days later the Williamsons and their maid suffered a similar fate. Following investigations, suspicion fell on a young sailor named John Williams, who lodged with Mrs Vermilloe at the Pear Tree public house. He was arrested and consigned to Coldbath Fields Prison, where he was later found dead in suspicious circumstances. Although his guilt was never established, Williams was deemed to have committed the crimes, and his body, after being paraded around Wapping, was buried at the crossroads of Cannon Street Road and Back Alley, now Cable Street, on New Year's Eve 1811, with a stake driven through his heart. The remains were later excavated when the road was rebuilt, and for a time the skull was an exhibit at the pub on the corner.

● Walk down toward the Highway.

4. St George-in-the-East was completed in 1723, one of three East End churches designed by the architect Nicholas Hawksmoor. It became a new parish church for Wapping Stepney, and one of the rectors of St George's in its early days was Dr Herbert Mayo. He took a keen interest in seafarers, especially black seamen, and one of his curates noted: 'I suppose no clergyman in England ever baptised so many black men and mulatoes.' The churchyard, which has been converted into a garden, has some very interesting gravestones, and contains a monument to the Raine family. The ruins of the Nature Study Museum are in the south-east corner. The church barely survived the Blitz, but the exterior walls are still standing, and there is a new chapel within the outer shell. An exciting find was the discovery of the Marr family tombstone, now lying in the boiler room

Henry Raine's monument and family vault, St George-in-the-East churchyard.

of the church. The stone was discovered by the rector when clearing some of the old graves, and having deciphered the name Marr on one side, he decided to store it away. In fact, when the stone was turned over and carefully cleaned, most of the original epitaph was revealed.

5. Jamrach's Shop (site only) on the Highway stood opposite Artichoke Hill. The proprietor also kept animals in Betts Street. Charles Jamrach was a wild animal importer, who came from Germany in the mid-19th century to open a branch of his father's business. There were several incidents when animals escaped, including a tiger and a python, but Jamrach always managed to recapture them. He died in 1891, and was succeeded by his son. The business closed in 1925.

The entrance to Wilton's music hall, Wellclose Square.

1859 with a variety of entertainment, but from being a high class venue, the music hall soon degenerated, with lurid stories being told of the dangers of falling prey to degraded women, being plied with drink, robbed and thrown into the river. In 1885 the premises were bought by the Methodists and the Old Mahogany Bar was a used as a hall and Temperance pub until 1956. Following the GLC's decision to demolish it, the British Music Hall Society fought to preserve the building, and with the help of Sir John Betjeman and local organisations, were successful in saving it. After a chequered history, opera productions are again being staged, although the hall still requires extensive refurbishment to restore it to its former glory.

● Return to the Highway.

10. Virginia Street Chapel (site only), the first Catholic place of worship in the East End, started life in the Windmill public house in Rosemary

Warehouses in Virginia Street, site of the Catholic chapel.

Lane, first mentioned in 1765. In 1780 the Gordon rioters destroyed the chapel, which was later rebuilt. A predominantly Irish Catholic population of around 14,000 lived in this area, working in the rag trade or in the docks. By 1849 the chapel was totally inadequate and a new chapel was built in what is now Sutton Street.

11. 29 Ratcliff Highway, on the south side of the Highway, almost opposite the junction with Betts Street, was the shop owned by Timothy Marr, a linen draper. On the night of Saturday 7 December 1811, after serving his customers late into the night, he and his shop-boy James Gowan began tidying up. His wife Celia was feeding the baby, Timothy, in the basement kitchen. Just before midnight Marr gave his servant girl Margaret Jewell a pound note to pay the baker's bill and buy some fresh oysters. Having found both the oyster shop and the baker's closed, Margaret returned to the shop, which now stood in darkness, and rang and knocked to no avail. The watchman and the pawnbroker next door came to her assistance, and found Timothy and Celia Marr, the baby and James Gowan all brutally murdered. The Thames River Police were immediately summoned, and a search for the murder weapon revealed a heavy iron mallet or maul, used by ship's carpenters, covered with blood and fragments of hair. The murders shocked the whole of London. John Williams, a sailor, was arrested for the crimes.

The vaults in Tobacco Dock.

12. Tobacco Dock, designed by Daniel Alexander, and built 1811–13, once stored skins, tobacco, spices and tea. The warehouses became redundant when the docks closed and were converted into a shopping centre, which unfortunately did not capture the shoppers' imaginations. Two replica ships are moored by the dock. There are two statues here which

St John the Evangelist Church, Scandrett Street, Wapping.

17. Turner's Old Star Pub has been so named because it is thought that the painter William Turner once bought the Old Star Tavern and gave it to one of his many mistresses, Sophia Booth. On his visits he passed himself off as Mr Booth, but he was so short and fat the locals nicknamed him 'Puggy Booth'. However, although there are elements of truth in the story, there are doubts as to whether this was in fact the pub. Turner was known to have owned The Ship and Bladebone in New Gravel Lane.

- **Walk through Wapping Gardens into Green Bank.**

18. St Patrick's Roman Catholic Church was built in 1880 for the Irish immigrants who worked for the docks and made up a third of Wapping's population by the mid-1800s. St Patrick's School in Red Lion Street was first mentioned in 1806, and the parish dates from 1871.

- **Turn left into Scandrett Street, on the right of which is the old churchyard.**

19. St John the Evangelist Church became the parish church of Wapping in 1694. It was first built as a chapel of ease for St Dunstan's, and was consecrated in 1617. The first church stood in the north-west part of the present churchyard, but it was poorly constructed in marshy ground and by 1760 the church had been rebuilt, with the school next door to it. The records of St John of Wapping show that, as at St George-in-the-East, large numbers of black seamen were baptised there. The 18th-century rector Dr Francis Willis was George III's doctor during his years of mental instability. George was also said to have secretly married local resident Hannah Lightfoot in 1759, before he became king. St John's Church was almost totally destroyed during the Blitz and only the church tower remains standing. The school has been turned into private apartments.

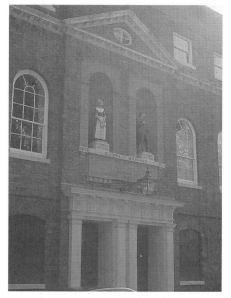
St John's Charity School, Scandrett Street.

- **Turn right into Wapping High Street.**

20. Wapping High Street was a single track road, which linked quays near the Tower with warehouses in Shadwell. John Stow called it 'a filthy straight passage', and it earned its name 'Sailor Town' from the many sailors' houses, brothels and taverns that lined the route. It was an ideal place for pirates to fence their ill-gotten booty, from silks to spices taken off merchant ships on distant trade routes.

21. The Town of Ramsgate, Wapping Old Stairs, is on the site of a 17th-century pub, which took its name in 1688 from the fishermen of Ramsgate who came up the Thames to Wapping Old Stairs, one of a number of flights of stairs giving access to the river. By 1750 the High Street had 36 taverns, but only the Town of Ramsgate survives.

22. Wapping Pier Head has a number of elegant houses built for dock officials in 1811. No.3 is the Customs House.

- **Walk back eastwards down Wapping High Street.**

23. Reardon Path, by Wapping New Stairs, was once Anchor and Hope Lane and the site of the Red Cow tavern. The notorious Judge Jeffries, who once condemned 330 to death at once for rebelling against James II, was arrested here. The 'Hanging' or 'Bloody' Jeffries secretly arranged to escape to France in 1688, but having stopped at the tavern for some liquid refreshment, he was recognised and mobbed. Saved by the militia, he was taken to the Tower, where he died, aged 40, of kidney stones.

24. Wapping Police Station was set up on the High Street, and the Marine Police formed here in 1798 was the world's first regular police force. They patrolled the river in rowing boats to guard merchant ships against the large scale pilferage that was a regular feature along this stretch of the water.

25. The Captain Kidd pub on Wapping High Street overlooks Execution Dock, the place where pirates were hanged until 1830. They were hanged and left for three tides to wash over them. At times, up to 100 criminals would be strung up and left to die on the gallows. It is supposedly haunted by the ghost of Captain James Kidd, who was hanged for piracy and murder in 1701, when he was 56 years old. The Admiralty considered him such an important catch that they tarred his corpse and left it swinging from a gibbet at Tilbury, where for years it was a constant reminder to other buccaneers of the fate that could befall them.

- **Continue up Wapping High Street, past the underground station and turn left.**

26. Garnet Street, formerly New Gravel Lane, (site only) some 300 yards east of Old Gravel Lane, was the scene of the next horrific crime 12 days after the Marrs were murdered. Mr and Mrs Williamson had been licencees of the King's Arms at 81 New Gravel Lane for 15 years and were well-known and respected. They lived with their granddaughter Kitty Stillwell, a middle-aged servant Bridget Harrington, and a young lodger named John Turner. On 19 December 1811, at about 11.30pm, there was a great commotion at the King's Arms, and John Turner was seen hanging from knotted sheets out of the window, shrieking, 'murder, murder!' He had apparently seen the murderers bending over Williamson's body and had made his escape. He fell into the arms of the watchman, still shouting incoherently. The other watchmen and neighbours then broke down the door, to find the Williamsons and Bridget Harrington dead with the most appalling injuries. Kitty Stillwell was fast asleep upstairs.

- **Walk up Garnet Street to the Highway, cross over and walk through Dellow Street, back to Shadwell station.**

Walk 2
Chinese Limehouse

From the City of London, travellers would pass along Ratcliff Highway, now the Highway, through Narrow Street, originally Fore Street, which connected Ratcliff to Limehouse. Narrow Street led into Limehouse Causeway, which continued along into Pennyfields, High Street Poplar and on to Blackwall. Lime Hurst, Lime Host and then Lime House were the names given to the hamlet where, from the 14th century, limekilns along the riverbanks processed lime for use as plaster in the construction of wooden buildings. The area bears little resemblance to the hamlet which flourished at this time, or indeed the small village whose parish church St Anne's dominated the skyline, and was a landmark for ships rounding the bend of the Isle of Dogs.

St Anne's Church, designed by Nicholas Hawksmoor, was built between 1714 and 1730. The village of Limehouse grew up around its parish church, but the only surviving village street is Newell Street, formerly Church Row. Wealthy merchants, ships' captains, maritime officials and other public servants settled here from the 15th century onwards, although very little evidence remains of their houses. The main hub of industrial life was situated along the riverside and the Limehouse Cut, where there were boatyards where boats and barges were built and repaired, small factories, rope manufactories, smoke holes for curing fish, a large brewery and even a porcelain factory. This idyllic lifestyle was to disappear with the construction of the West India Docks.

The East India Company, whose yard at Blackwall dated from 1612, probably contributed more than anything else to the familiar sight of the foreign seaman or lascar, found wandering the streets of Poplar and Limehouse, largely ignored by the local community. Lascars were paid half or less in wages, and were simply paid off at London and left to find their own way home on a ship returning to the East. Many of these lascars stayed in and around Limehouse and Poplar and the scandal of foreign sailors dying of starvation and cold in the streets by the docks soon demanded a solution. In 1857 the Strangers Home in West India Dock Road, built to house foreign seamen, was opened by Prince Albert. Besides Chinese, there were large numbers of Burmese, Malay and Indian seamen, as well as those from the Caribbean. There was also a substantial Scandinavian population, for which a Danish Church was built in King (Ming) Street, and a Scandinavian Mission in Garford Street.

Chinatown in Limehouse existed from 1860 to 1950, although even at its height there were no more than 4,000 Chinese living there. It was in part thanks to Victorian and Edwardian writers that the public's attention was drawn to Chinese Limehouse. Charles Dickens often stayed in Limehouse at his uncle's house in Church Row as a young boy, and he later used the streets and people he met in his novels. He was also said to have written his novel *Our Mutual Friend* while residing at The Grapes in Narrow Street. The opening scene in *The Mystery of Edwin Drood* is set in an opium den in Limehouse, and the horrors of opium smoking are powerfully conveyed. In *The Picture of Dorian Gray*, Oscar Wilde has his protagonist coming to

Limehouse in search of 'opium dens, where one could buy oblivion, dens of horror where the memory of old sins could be destroyed by the madness of sins that were new.'

Thomas Burke's tales of Limehouse, which both fascinated and entertained the new cinema audiences, put Chinese Limehouse in the international spotlight. Burke (1887–1945) was born in London, and having been orphaned when a few months old, was sent to his uncle in Gill Street, Limehouse, with whom he lived until the age of nine. Burke wrote around 30 novels, and a book of poems, *The Song Book of Quong Lee* (1920). His first novel, *Limehouse Nights*, published in August 1917, opens with a tragedy, *The Chink and the Child*. This chapter was adapted by D.W. Griffiths and *Broken Blossoms*, starring Lilian Gish and Donald Crisp, was a Hollywood hit. Thomas Burke went on to script several of his novels for films. *Limehouse Nights* was a hit movie for George Raft and Anna May Wong, as was *The Mysterious Mr Moto* (1938) with Peter Lorre.

Sax Rohmer's Fu Manchu novels, however, turned the inscrutable oriental into a sinister evil monster.

At the turn of the 20th century opium could be bought and sold over the counter and was smoked fairly openly in Limehouse. In 1908 an Act of Parliament attempted to inhibit the sale of opium and the London County Council passed a bye-law in 1909 whereby lodging houses could lose their licences if it was found that the premises were used for opium smoking.

In 1919 a wave of anti-Chinese riots swept the East End, fuelled by stories of a white slave trade and fears of the 'yellow peril'. Following a period of relative quiet, in 1930 Limehouse inexplicably witnessed further police raids on puck-apu gambling dens and opium sellers. Possession of opium often resulted in a prison sentence and deportation, which was especially hard on those Chinese men who had married English women and had families. Chinese women did not initially come to the East End in any significant numbers. Annie Lai, an English woman

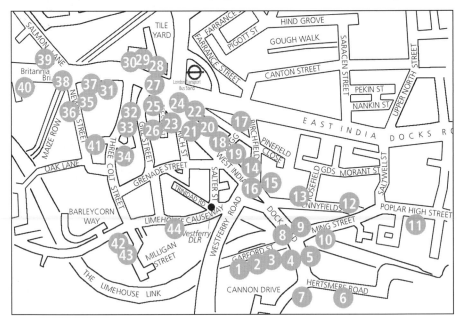

married to Yuen Sing Lai, a Cantonese who was eventually deported, could remember only three Chinese women in Limehouse in the 1930s. A new law making it illegal to sign on a Chinese crew in any British port also contributed to the decrease in the Chinese community between the two World Wars.

Besides opium dens, gambling was a popular pastime in Limehouse. Puck-apu, very similar to our National Lottery, was carried on all day in the shops in Pennyfields and Limehouse Causeway. Papers printed with 80 symbols (or numbers) were sold for a shilling to customers, who marked off 10 numbers. Every hour numbers were drawn, and £500 could be won if all 10 numbers matched, with corresponding prizes for 9 or less.

In 1934, in an attempt to disperse the Chinese settled in Limehouse, a plan by the Stepney Borough Council to widen Limehouse Causeway and Pennyfields succeeded in clearing many of the shops and houses that gave the area its character. The Blitz then took its toll, and several Chinese names appear on the fatality lists in September 1940. Many were buried in a mass grave in Tower Hamlets cemetery, as no one came forward to claim the bodies.

Post-war development in the area around Pennyfields completed the destruction of Chinatown in Limehouse. Widening of the West India Dock Road, Pennyfields and Limehouse Causeway, and the Limehouse Link necessitated the removal of rows of shops, restaurants and several large blocks of flats. To find traces of what was once a thriving dockside hamlet takes a bit of exploring and a lot of imagination. It is truly a treasure hunt, and discovering little gems of the past tucked away down a side alley away from the main roads is a reward well worth the time and effort.

In Search of Chinese Limehouse

The walk begins at Westferry Docklands Station. The Docklands Light Railway runs from Bank underground station, or Tower Hill station on the refurbished Fenchurch Street to Blackwall line.

● **Cross over the road ahead as you come down the stairs and walk along West Ferry Road, turning left into Garford Street.**

1. St Peter's Church (site only), built in 1866, stood on the right side of Garford Street. The church was declared redundant in November 1969, and the parish was united with St Anne's Limehouse in 1971.
2. Constables Cottages are a row of houses constructed in 1817 for the dock police who guarded the West India Docks. The sergeant's dwelling in the middle is the largest.

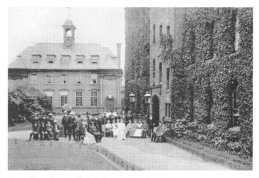

Scandinavian Sailors' Home, Garford Street.

3. The Scandinavian Sailors' Temperance Home in Garford Street was one of the many hostels for seafarers built in the East End of London. In 1875 Agnes Hedenstrom, a missionary from the Swedish Free Church, came to the East End to work among seafarers, preaching to Scandinavian sailors whose ships docked in the port. In 1888, as Madam Agnes Welin (having married in the interim), the indomitable missionary opened her Scandinavian Sailors' Home. The imposing building, which dates from 1902, and its adjoining Greig House, a beautiful red-brick building with a copper-clad clock tower, constructed in 1911 and used by the officers of the Swedish Merchant fleet, is now occupied by the Salvation Army and run as a hostel for homeless men.

● **From Garford Street turn right toward what was once the West India Dock Gates.**

4. The Dockmaster's House dates from 1807 and was designed by Thomas Morris, engineer to the West India Dock Company. It was first used as an excise office and then was converted into a tavern, the Jamaica Hotel, for travellers disembarking at the docks. When the Port of London Authority acquired the building it became the dock manager's office. It is now a rather upmarket Indian restaurant.

5. The West India Dock Gates stood in front of the sugar warehouses, controlling the entrance into the docks, with a central pillar on which stood the statue of Robert Milligan, the promoter and first Deputy Chairman of the West India Dock Company. There was another entrance further along in the form of an arch leading into the docks, just wide enough to allow a horse and cart through. Above the arch was the model of the ship *Hibbert*. The arch was demolished in 1932, and the model was taken to Poplar recreation ground. After World War Two an attempt was made to shift the ship to Poplar Library, but the model crumbled and had to be scrapped.

6. The sugar warehouses in the West India Docks were designed by George Gwilt and his son George. They were constructed in 1802, but only a third of the buildings were left standing after the devastation inflicted on the docks during the Blitz. They are exceptional examples of surviving dock warehouse architecture, and have recently been converted into luxury apartments and a leisure complex, and will also house the museum in Docklands.

7. The Ledger Building, down Hertsmere Road, has been refurbished with the sugar warehouses. A new entrance was built in the year 2000 and Milligan's statue has been reinstated here.

8. The Railway Tavern (site only), popularly known as Charlie Brown's pub, stood on the corner of West India Dock Road by the dock gates opposite the West India Dock Station of the London and Blackwall Railway. The pub was built in around 1845, and Charlie Brown became landlord in 1894. He ran a lucrative side business buying whatever sailors returning home had to offer for sale, from Ming vases and jade statues to curios of every description. His pub was crammed with priceless artefacts, which he displayed to the public. During the first decades of the 20th century society folk came down to Limehouse to buy and smoke opium. Tragically, a young actress named Billie Carleton was found dead nearby from a drugs overdose. Some time later, among Charlie Brown's exhibits was the clay pipe Billie

Carleton smoked on the night she died. When Charlie Brown died in June 1932, thousands of people turned out for his funeral, one of the largest ever seen in Limehouse. Charlie Brown's pub was demolished in 1989 to make way for the Limehouse Link road.

9. The Blue Posts public house (site only) stood opposite the Railway Tavern, and the landlord was the son of Charlie Brown and was also named Charles. Following his father's death, Charlie displayed many of the antiques and curios inherited from his father at the Blue Posts. His sister and her husband took over the Railway Tavern, which became known as Charlie Brown's pub. He later moved to the Roundabout pub in Woodford, but the pub was demolished when the motorway was constructed, although the junction is still referred to as Charlie Brown's roundabout.

10. The Danish Lutheran Church (site only), built in 1877 in King Street, now Ming Street, was mainly attended by Danish sailors and their families, and was associated with the Marlborough House Chapel at St James's Palace. The building held around 200 people. In front of the altar hung a model ship made by an old captain in Denmark and presented to the church after an exhibition in Copenhagen in 1888. The service books in the church were a gift from the then Princess of Wales, later Queen Alexandra, and signed 'For our Danish Church in Poplar – Alexandra'.

11. No.48 Poplar High Street (site only) was the Chinese Freemason Society Chee Kong Tong. Given the secrecy surrounding the Freemasons, it is not surprising that we know very little about this society, although a search through the records for evidence of Chinese and English mixed marriages did reveal that Fu Chai, secretary of the Chinese Freemasons' Lodge, registered his marriage to Lena Blair on 23 May 1931. Yuen Sing Lai, who married an English woman named Annie, was an influential member during the 1920s. Yuen Sing Lai was later deported, leaving Annie and her children to fend for themselves.

12. Pennyfields, a predominately Chinese area, home to a few hundred Chinese families, was cleared in 1934 as part of Stepney's slum clearance programme, and road expansions in the 1990s have left virtually nothing of the old Pennyfields. Seamen from Shanghai and Ningpo tended to settle in

Silver Lion Court, Pennyfields, Limehouse.

Pennyfields, Amoy Place and Poplar High Street, while those from Canton settled in Limehouse Causeway, West India Dock Road and Gill Street. The Chinese settled here at the beginning of the 20th century and formed a thriving business community. By 1918 there were 182 Chinese men living in Pennyfields, of whom nine were married to English women. By the 1920s the total Chinese population of Limehouse was around 4,000. Silver Lion Court, with the Silver Lion pub at No.65, was approximately halfway up Pennyfields, on the north side of the street.

The Rose and Crown in Pennyfields, Limehouse.

13. The Rose and Crown Pub in Pennyfields was run by Queenie Watts and her husband in the 1970s and early 1980s. Queenie was a famous jazz singer and a successful TV actress, starring in the long-running series *Romany Jones* as the wife of Arthur Mullard. The first pub she ran was the Iron Bridge Tavern on East India Dock Road. Queenie Watts died of cancer in 1983 at the age of 56. The pub is now a private residence.

14. Ting Kee Refreshments (site only) was next door to the Oporto pub, at 39–41 West India Dock Road. It was the best known and probably the largest Chinese restaurant in Limehouse during the 1930s, and probably closed down sometime during World War Two.

15. The Commercial Tavern stood on the corner of Pennyfields and Birchfield Street, opposite the Oporto. Daniel Farson wrote in his memoirs *Limehouse Days* of going into the Commercial for a drink sometime during the 1950s, and hearing more Chinese than English spoken.

16. West India Dock Road (south side) has been completely obliterated by the widening of the road in the building of the Limehouse Link. Mr Lo-Cheong and Mrs Farmer once ran an

Looking down West India Dock Road toward Charlie Brown's pub.

Old Friends Restaurant in Mandarin Street. Later the family also opened the New Friends and the Friendly House. The Chinese Mission was at 92 West India Dock Road, and was one of several missions opened during the 1920s and 1930s, to bring Christianity to the Chinese community. There was also a Burmese restaurant and several other Chinese restaurants and establishments.

17. The Chinese Sunday School & Chun Yee Society on the corner of East India Dock Road and Birchfield Street is one of the last remnants of the Limehouse Chinese connection. The Chun Yee Society was previously at No.37 Pennyfields.

● **Walk through Amoy Place and Rugg Street, the site of Stepney laundry. This was perhaps the place where one 'Got those kind of Limehouse Chinese Laundry Blues!'**

18. The Salvation Army Hostel, the building next door to the car park of the Limehouse police station, has a plaque stating that the first Salvation Army Hostel was opened here in 1888. There are some interesting sailing craft bronzes on the building.

19. The Limehouse police station was from where the police fought a relentless battle in the 1920s and 1930s to contain the selling and smoking of opium. Their raids on opium dens and Chinese homes made headline news.

20. West India House was opened in November 1946 by the then Prime Minister Clement Attlee, MP for Limehouse. It was originally the site of the Strangers Home for Asiatics,

Africans and South Sea Islanders, which was opened in 1857 by Prince Albert. The plight of lascars, employed on ships trading with the Far East, caused grave concern in the 1850s. Paid off after docking at London, they were often found wandering the streets around the docks, dying of cold and starvation. Henry Venn then launched an appeal for funds to open a hostel for lascars. By the 1930s the home was unoccupied, and in 1938 it was taken over by Stepney Council and used to house families made homeless by their slum clearance project. The building was subsequently demolished and the present block of flats was built on the site.

21. The Ship's Chandlers building is dated 1860, and until a few years ago was the office of Coubro and Scrutton's. Following their departure the building has lain empty. At one time it was used by the Salvation Army and had an unusual ceiling painted by them.

22. No.7 West India Dock Road was the home of a Swedish captain, Baron Eric Leijonhjelm. From about 1897 his widow Baroness Leijonhjelm kept a small evangelical meeting room open. This imperious little old lady became a famous figure locally, and her establishment was listed in turn as the Scandinavian Mission Room, the Finnish Sailors Mission Room, and in 1927 as the East London Seamen's Mission, when it was combined with No.9 next door, previously a dining room run by Mrs Johanna Tarry.

23. The Marine Officers' Residential Club for Merchant Navy Officers was housed in the elegant building on the corner of Rich Street, now converted into private apartments. Half the cost of the club was met by Passmore Edwards. Further down Rich Street were the offices of the Inland Revenue, Customs and Excise and the dreaded National Assistance Board.

Nos 7–9 West India Dock Road, home of Baroness Leijonhjelm.

24. The Great Eastern Hotel (site only), built in 1862, stood on the corner of the junction of East India Dock Road and West India Dock Road. Among its notable guests were the king of Siam and Joseph Conrad. The hotel was later an Irish pub, The Londoner, until the early

The Junction at Limehouse, with the Great Eastern Hotel on the right.

1990s when it had a brief spell as The Lipstick. It was demolished shortly afterwards and a painted façade now hides the site.

25. The British and Foreign Sailors Hostel, which stands at the junction of West India Dock Road and Commercial Road, also housed the King Edward VII Nautical College and was opened in 1901. The Tower Hamlets Chinese Association now has its office here. The hostel was referred to locally as the 'stack o' bricks', because of the distinctive red and white bands on its frontage. There are several interesting features on the front entrance of the building.

26. Gill Street is a little turning off Commercial Road past the Sailors' Hostel, where Thomas Burke, author of *Limehouse Nights* and other books, lived with his uncle for the first nine years of his life. Gill Street was home to several sea captains over the years, and there is an interesting headstone in Tower Hamlets cemetery, which bears the name of Captain Gill of Limehouse, and at least two other sea captains.

27. Commercial Road, constructed in 1810, meets with East and West India Dock Roads and Burdett Road at a major junction at Limehouse. In order to pay for the road, tolls were levied on vehicles passing through. A toll house stood at this junction until 1871, when tolls were abolished.

28. Francis & C. Walters, undertakers at 811 Commercial Road, were known as Francis J. Walters at the beginning of the 20th century. The establishment is over 200 years old and its distinctive frontage was refurbished in the 1990s with the help of English Heritage.

29. The Star of the East pub, situated a few doors away from the undertakers, has an imposing façade, a fine example of pub architecture. A pair of gas lamps survives on the pavement outside the premises.

30. The Chinatown Restaurant with its curved frontage is one of the little gems of Limehouse. The cellars of the restaurant extend under Commercial Road toward the church, and legend has it that they once gave access to a tunnel or passage that continued to the river.

- **Cross over the Commercial Road to the church.**

31. The parish church of St Anne's at Limehouse was designed by Nicholas Hawksmoor, and was built between 1714 and 1730. The main features of the church were its dazzling white stonework and the great height of its clocktower, which at one time was the highest in London. The church is precisely aligned to the central axis of the Royal Naval College at Greenwich, from where it is clearly visible. The church was damaged by a serious fire in 1850 and major refurbishment was carried out by P.C. Hardwick between 1851 and 1853, retaining much of Hawksmoor's plan and structure. The exterior of the church was restored in 1985-90, and further restoration work was completed in the 1990s.

Chinatown Restaurant, Commercial Road, Limehouse.

The War Memorial in St Anne's churchyard.

32. The Five Bells and Bladebone Pub in Three Colt Street dates from 1803, when it was known as the Five Bells. The name refers to the custom of ringing five bells at 2.30pm, when the docks closed. In 1845 the name was changed to the Five Bells and Bladebone, when a whale's bladebone found in the docks was brought to the pub for display.

33. Limehouse Church Institute, the church hall for St Anne's Church, opposite, was built in 1903. A substantial building, it was refurbished in 1989 and converted into private apartments.

34. Brunswick Methodist Chapel (site only) in Three Colt Street was built in 1832, and stood adjacent to the old Limehouse Station on the Fenchurch Street to Blackwall Line, constructed in 1845. There was a burial ground at the

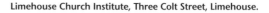

Limehouse Church Institute, Three Colt Street, Limehouse.

St Anne's parish church, Limehouse, viewed from Newell Street.

back of the chapel, popular with dissenters in the area. However, by 1895, many of the well-to-do families had moved out of the area. The Seamen's Mission, which moved from Commercial Road, took over the premises. A sailors' bible class was started, which proved to be a turning point for the chapel. There was a flourishing sunday school, a drift children's meeting on Thursday night, often attended by over 1,000 children, a cripples' parlour, a factory girls bible class and a social club. In 1931 Dr Harold Oatley from the London Hospital set up a Sunday school for Chinese children. Dr Oatley, who later became a distinguished surgeon, ran the children's mission with his wife Win until their deaths. In 1937 the Brunswick Chapel was condemned as unsafe, and in January 1939, the Shaftesbury Society was informed that the Limehouse Ragged School was closed.

35. The Rectory at No.5 Newell Street stands on the site of No.12 Church Row, the home of Christopher Huffam, godfather of Charles Dickens. From about 1823, when the Dickens family had fallen on hard times, the young Charles paid regular visits to his godfather. During these visits Huffam would take Charles with him on his travels around Limehouse, and many of the places, streets and houses he pointed out to his godson found their way into the novelist's works.

36. The Prince of Wales Sea Training Hostel, diagonally opposite the rectory, opened on 25 February 1920. The hostel trained boys for the Merchant Navy, and was built and run by the British and Foreign Sailors' Society, whose headquarters were in Commercial Road, at the junction with West India Dock Road.

37. Limehouse Town Hall, on the corner of Newell Street and Commercial Road, was originally the Vestry Hall of Limehouse parish. The Town Hall was the scene of the election of Clement Attlee as Labour MP for Limehouse in 1922.

38. Limehouse Cut, spanned by the Britannia Bridge, goes under the road here and is the oldest canal

Limehouse Town Hall, Commercial Road.

Limehouse Cut, viewed from Burdett Road.

in London. It was built in 1770 to link the River Lea at Bow with the Thames at Limehouse, and was intended to save the heavy barges bringing produce down from Hertfordshire the long journey down the Lea and round the Isle of Dogs to reach the Pool of London.

The Empire Memorial Hostel, at the corner of Salmon Lane and Commercial Road.

Clement Attlee's statue outside Limehouse Library, Commercial Road.

39. The Empire Memorial Hostel, at the junction of Salmon Lane and Commercial Road, was built in memory of the 12,000 merchant seamen who died in World War One. It opened in 1924 as a hostel for sailors. An extension was built in 1933. Known as Prince's Lodge, the hostel had become rather dilapidated by the 1980s. It was closed by the local authorities and the building sold to private developers for conversion into luxury apartments. It is now known as The Mission. Salmon Lane, once known as Sermon's Lane, connected Limehouse with St Dunstan's parish church. Salmon Lane is mentioned by Dickens in an article called *One Dinner a Week*, an account of his visit to the New Cottage Mission Hall at 67 Salmon Lane, where Irish stew dinners were provided for about 200 people every Wednesday. Each diner had to provide their own plate and spoon.

40. Limehouse Library, a short distance down Commercial Road, has a statue of Clement Attlee, MP for Limehouse and the first Labour Prime Minister after World War Two.

• Return to Newell Street and the Mitre.

41. Mitre Schools (site only) were used in 1876 by the Limehouse Ragged School, which was opened in 1856 by Burnett Tabrum in Three Colt Street. Although most Ragged Schools in the country closed prior to World War One, following the advent of compulsory education

for all children, the work of the Ragged School at Limehouse continued at the Brunswick Chapel right up to 1938.

- **Continue through to Three Colt Lane and Narrow Street.**

42. Dunbar's Wharf, Narrow Street, was owned by Duncan Dunbar. Dunbar, who settled in Limehouse in 1780, built ships in Calcutta for his trade. He lived in the house next-door to the wharf, 138 Narrow Street. His son, also called Duncan, built a fine mansion, Howrah House, in East India Dock Road in 1790. This house was later bought in 1881 by the nuns and became the Convent of the Faithful Companions, and a select girls' school.

- **Walk down Three Colt Street to Limekiln Dock.**

Limekiln Wharf, with the Limehouse Door on the right.

43. The Limehouse Kiln Dock at Limehouse Hole has been imaginatively refurbished, and includes a replica of the Limehouse Kiln door. The original door was salvaged and taken to the Ragged School Museum in Copperfield Road. Limehouse got its name from the lime kilns or lime oasts, where lime brought up from Kent was burnt, the earliest reference to which was in 1362.

44. Limehouse Causeway, an ancient pathway, was so narrow that only one cart or van could get through in any direction. It was inhabited mainly by the Cantonese, while Pennyfields was the home of men from Shanghai. All this vanished when Stepney Borough Council decided upon their 'slum clearance', and tore down the rickety, sloping houses, all interconnected by tiny alleyways and arches.

- **The Causeway takes you back past Mandarin Street to Westferry Station.**

Walk 3
Poplar and the Docks

Poplar was part of the manor of Stepney in Domesday times, one of the many hamlets which grew up along the River Thames. The name has been found spelt as Popeler, Popler and Popelar. One of the theories was that the name referred to the number of poplar trees growing in the area, but there is no real evidence to support this. It is possible that a single poplar tree grew on the high ground north of the Isle of Dogs, visible from the river, which provided a sighting point for travellers.

The first inhabitants of Poplar appear to have lived in a settlement at Blackwall and along the High Street. The only route from London was via Ratcliffe Highway, through Limehouse Causeway, High Street Poplar and on to Blackwall Yard. At one time there were upwards of 27 inns and taverns along High Street Poplar, and a further 15 at Blackwall.

The only route north was via North Street, from the junction with the High Street at the White Horse pub. This section is now called Saltwell Street. The road going northwards was about half a mile long, turning into a cart track and losing itself on Bow Common. The other route, to the east, was Bow Lane, now Bazely Street, which continued northwards into what is now Ida Street, then curved around to join Robin Hood Lane. This was the extent of the hamlet of Poplar until the 18th century.

During the reign of Henry VIII, with the dissolution of the monasteries, the manor remained with the crown, but was eventually granted out to various worthy people. The manor of Poplar and the manor house of Poplar were owned separately. Sir Gilbert Dethick was granted the manor house and an acre of land in Poplar by Henry VIII. His son Sir William Dethick was born in Poplar in 1543, and was knighted by James I. William's son Henry Dethick was a prominent man in local affairs, and was Poplar's representative in the Stepney Vestry. He was also churchwarden in 1639, the year he died. The manor house then passed to various owners until in the 18th century it came into the possession of Jeremiah Shirbutt Wade. The original manor house was demolished in 1810 during the building of the East India Dock Road, and a new manor house was built on the opposite south side of the new road.

In 1601 the formation of the East India Company led to an increase of activity at Blackwall. In 1612 the company acquired a ship building yard and built depots, stores and houses for its officials. They also built almshouses and a chapel. Poplar Chapel, now St Matthias, was built in 1654 for the use of mariners in the service of the company, as a chapel of ease. In 1817 the parishioners of Poplar successfully appealed for a parish church and All Saints' Church was built, completed in 1823.

The main highway was High Street Poplar and there were 15 inns and houses of refreshment listed there in 1821. Robin Hood Lane had dwellings and stables, besides two warehouses and the East India Company's wagon shed. Blackwall too had several residential properties, besides the famous Blackwall Yard. Further south of Coldharbour was Folly House, with a large garden

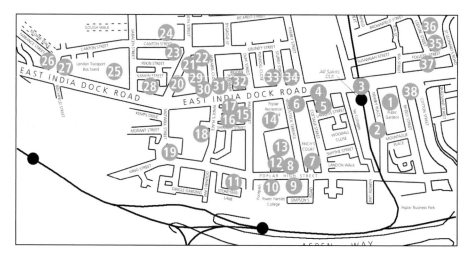

and landing place from the Thames. This was a popular tavern with a cock-pit. Later Yarrows set up their famous shipbuilding yard at Folly House.

The building of the new docks gave rise to a huge increase in population. The number of houses in the new parish of All Saints' in 1818 was quoted as 1,476, with 7,708 inhabitants. Three years later the census figures show 12,223 inhabitants living in 2,020 houses. In contrast, Bow had 2,349 inhabitants and 413 houses, while Bromley had 4,360 inhabitants and 903 houses. This increase in population was the direct result of the opening of the West and East India Docks, from 1800 onwards, as labourers who came to build the docks then stayed to work in them.

The East India Dock Road was soon to become the main highway connecting Commercial Road to the docks and continuing on to Canning Town. The company paid Mrs Wade £900 for the land and work started on the road in 1805. Running mainly through field and market gardens, it was lined with grand houses and shops. Some of these houses still exist, on the south-west side of the road. On the north side, only No.153 Palm Cottage, which was one of four houses, gives us a glimpse of the elegant dwellings constructed for ship-builders and sea-captains, as well as for those who serviced the ships in the docks.

Green's Home for Sailors is still standing, although it has been converted into apartments, and the gas cottages in Mallam Gardens are now sought-after residences. Of the six churches which stood in the East India Dock Road, only All Saints' survived the Blitz. All Hallows, St Stephen's, Bath Street Chapel, United Methodist (Lax's) and Trinity Church were all severely damaged and later demolished. Only Trinity Church was rebuilt as part of the Festival of Britain in 1951.

Poplar suffered tremendous damage during World War Two, although it did not escape its share of bombing during World War One either. On 13 June 1917 the little school in Upper North Street suffered a direct hit from a bomb dropped by a Gotha aircraft, killing 18 children.

So much of Poplar was demolished by enemy action, that when the Festival of Britain was planned, Poplar was part of the live architectural exhibition, with various architects invited to design blocks of flats and houses on what is now the Lansbury Estate, named after George Lansbury the popular councillor, mayor and Member of Parliament, who was so beloved of his community.

Today it is still possible to explore the streets and turnings of this large hamlet, and glimpse something of its magnificent past.

Poplar and the East India Dock Road

The walk starts at All Saints' Docklands Station. Alternatively, buses from Mile End underground are the D6 and D7.

1. All Saints' Church, in Newby Place, consecrated in 1823, was designed by Charles Hollis and built by Thomas Morris of Blackwall. The parish of All Saints' was created after the inhabitants of Poplar made a petition to Parliament in 1816. Until then it formed part of the parish of Stepney, with St Dunstan's the mother church.

2. Poplar Town Hall (site only) opposite, was built in 1870 on the site of the Watch House in Newby Place. The Town Hall was the scene of the famous Poplar Rates Dispute of 1920–1. The Poplar councillors, led by George Lansbury, declared shortly after their election that Poplar bore an intolerable burden of local taxes, having to levy the highest rates, while boroughs such as Westminster levied the lowest. Having refused to collect rates, the councillors were taken to court by the government, eventually being sentenced to a term of imprisonment. In September 1921, the councillors and aldermen, including five women, were taken to Brixton and Holloway prisons.

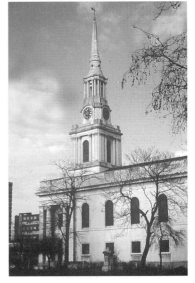

All Saints' parish church, Poplar.

Eventually, the government acceded to Poplar's demands, and rates were equalised across London. The word 'poplarism' entered the dictionary. There is a red plaque commemorating this event on a shop opposite the junction of Newby Place and East India Dock Road.

3. The East India Dock Road was built to provide access from Commercial Road to the East India Docks at Blackwall. In 1805 the dock company bought part of Mrs Wade's land for £900. One hundred years later the road was lined on either side with fine houses and shops. Some of these still exist despite the destruction of property during the Blitz: Green's

The plaque in East India Dock Road commemorating the Poplar Rates Dispute of 1921.

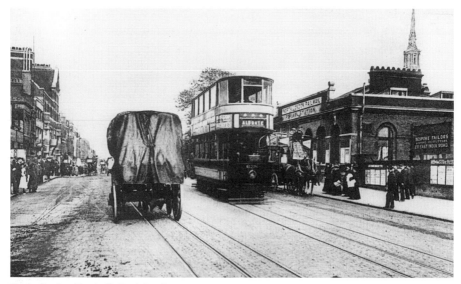

Poplar Station, East India Dock Road.

Home for Sailors, the Missions to Seamen, and the Queen Victoria Seamen's Rest survive. Of the churches All Saints' alone escaped serious damage. Trinity Church was rebuilt in a modern style. Lax's Church, All Hallows and St Stephen's were demolished.

4. Poplar Baths, built in 1856, was one of the first public baths and wash houses to be opened in London. It was replaced by new baths and a swimming pool in 1933, and finally closed in 1987.

5. Richard Green's statue, by the sculptor Edward Wyon, was erected in front of the baths in 1866. He is seated on a chair covered by a sailcloth, with his faithful dog Hector by his side. Richard Green took over from his father George Green and was a successful shipbuilder at Blackwall.

6. The Methodist Church (site only) was built on the corner of Woodstock Terrace, alongside an earlier Methodist chapel in Bath Street, which dated from the beginning of the Methodist Movement. John Wesley preached here in 1780. Later King George's Hall was built on the site. William Lax,

Richard Green's statue outside Poplar Baths.

flamboyant minister of the church for 35 years, was so well-known that people referred to the church as 'Lax's Church'. In 1934 J. Arthur Rank made a film about Lax's life. Revd Lax died in 1937 and Minnie, his wife, in 1943, shortly after the church was totally destroyed in a bombing raid.

- ## Walk down Woodstock Road to Poplar High Street.

7. Stocks Academy (site only) stood between Woodstock Terrace and Cottage Street. An imposing building, it had a large garden and three acres of land attached to it. A boarding and day school for young gentlemen, founded by John Stock, it flourished in the 1800s and probably closed in 1852–3. The name 'Woodstock' comes from Edward Wood Stock, landowner, grandson of John Stock. The Coroner's Court and Mortuary Office, on the corner of Cottage Street, dates to 1910 and is still in use.
8. The council offices, used as the Town Hall extension, date from the mid-19th century and are built of yellow and red brick and stone, with a distinctive gabled copper dome.

The interior of the council offices, Poplar High Street.

9. The Holy Child Settlement was founded at Tower Hill in 1893 by the Dowager Duchess of Newcastle. After her death in 1913, her assistant Miss Magdalen Walker took over and in 1919 the settlement moved to 130 Poplar High Street. Mother and baby clinics, marriage guidance counselling and Catholic care committee work, as well as a youth club, were among its activities. The building was destroyed during the Blitz and rebuilt in 1951. It is now a centre for Vietnamese Catholics.

Holy Child Settlement, Poplar High Street.

The old Poplar Library on Poplar High Street, once a School of Marine Engineering, now Tower Hamlets College. The site of Poplar Workhouse is on the far right.

10. Tower Hamlets College has recently been extended. Built by the London County Council in 1906 as the School of Marine Engineering, it later became Poplar Technical College.
11. The Poplar Workhouse (site only), in Stoneyard Lane, was demolished in 1960 and part of the site taken by Tower Hamlets College. A community and leisure centre now occupies the remaining land.
12. St Matthias Vicarage is an attractive 19th-century building with a coat of arms on the pediment. The remains of a Tudor well were discovered in the grounds.
13. St Matthias Church was originally the company chapel, built by the East India Company in 1654. The church was rebuilt in 1776 and refurbished in 1866. Following its closure in 1976 when the congregation was amalgamated with All Saints' Church, the building fell into disrepair, but was

St Matthias Church, Poplar Recreation Ground.

saved by English Heritage and the London Docklands Development Corporation (LDDC), who refurbished it to house a community centre. There are several monuments of interest within the church, to John Perry, George Green and other shipbuilders, although Flaxman's monument to George Steevens was removed for an exhibition in Cambridge and has not been replaced.

14. Poplar Recreation Park was laid out in 1867 on the site of the East India Company almshouses. The Angel Memorial commemorates the deaths of 18 children who were killed on 13 June 1917, when their school in Upper North Street received a direct hit from a bomb dropped by a Gotha aircraft during the first daylight air raid over London.

The Angel Memorial in Poplar Recreation Ground.

15. The Missions to Seamen Institute in Hale Street was built in the 1880s, but was acquired by the Gas Co-partnership, and remained with the Gas Company until after World War Two. It was then bought by St Mary and St Joseph's parish and renamed Pope John House, and was converted into a club and social centre in the 1960s. In the late 1990s the building was sold to a private developer. Manor Lodge on the corner of Hale Street recalls the site of the 19th century manor house.

16. The manor house of Poplar stood on the site of the present Duff Street, on the north side of East India Dock Road. It was granted to Sir Gilbert Dethick by Henry VIII, together with an acre of land. In the 18th century Jeremiah Wade owned the property, but by 1800 it was in a dilapidated condition and in 1810 it was pulled down during the building of the East India Dock Road and rebuilt on the south side opposite. Mrs Mary Wade, widow of Jeremiah Shirbutt Wade (d.1806), and her five daughters were then owners of the property. Elizabeth Chrisp Willis, Susannah Grundy, Sarah Kerby, Sophia Duff and Catherine Wade and their parents have given their names to at least 14 streets in the area. By the 1850s the manor house was occupied by a Thomas Westhorpe and later rented by Dr M. Corner, surgeon. In 1933 the house was sold to the Commercial Gas Company and demolished.

17. Mallam Gardens consists of three rows of cottages built for employees of the Gas Board on the site of the manor house. Two of the original gas lamps still survive in the lanes between the cottages.

18. Holy Family School in Wade's Place is the oldest Catholic school in London. It was founded as Wade Street School by Father Barber in 1816. The small school room was used as a chapel for Irish Catholics, and the present school yard was the burial ground. From 1882 the school was run by the Sisters of the Faithful Companions of Jesus. Miss Ellen Lynn, who retired in 1947, spent 60 years at the school, 47 of them as class mistress in the Infants School.

● **Walk down Poplar High Street and turn into Saltwell Street.**

19. The White Horse pub at the corner of Saltwell Street and Poplar High Street has a fascinating story dating back to the 18th century. In the early 1740s the landlord of the

White Horse was James Howes, who, together with Mrs Howes, ran a successful and prosperous tavern. The 'couple' were in fact two women from Limehouse, Mary East and a Miss How. Mary was born in around 1715, her companion a year later. Having both been disappointed in love they decided to spend their lives together, and live as man and wife. A Mrs Bentley recognised Mary, and with an accomplice, James Barwick, black-mailed her for several years. Eventually, Mary sought the help of her neighbour Mr Williams, who laid a trap for Mrs Bentley. The blackmailers were caught and in October 1766 were sent to Bridewell Prison. Mary East then lived as a female until her death on 4 June 1780. Although there several variations to the story, it is known from parish records that James Howes had several properties in Poplar and

The White Horse pub at the corner of Saltwell Street and Poplar High Street.

was Headborough and an Overseer of the Poor in 1752. Mary East was buried in Poplar Chapel and the headstone read 'Mary East, the woman-man of Poplar'. The pub was rebuilt in 1935, and has undergone further refurbishment. It has a fine plaque of a white horse on the exterior and the statue of the white horse, which is Grade II listed, still stands outside.

- **Continue up Saltwell Street and cross over to the other side of East India Dock Road.**

Junction of Upper North Street and East India Dock Road.

20. Upper North Street was the only route north from the junction with the High Street at the White Horse pub. The road going northwards was about half a mile long, turning into a cart track, and losing itself on Bow Common.

21. George Green's Almshouses were built in the 1840s by Green for poor women and widows in Poplar. In 1895 there were 21 residents, aged between 59 and 91 years. The building now contains flats for single women and is administered by the Springboard Housing Trust.

George Green's Almshouses, Upper North Street.

22. Upper North Street School was the scene of a devastating bomb attack during World War One, when on 13 June 1917, Gotha aircraft, returning from a bombing raid on London, continued to drop bombs along their return route, over Limehouse and Poplar. A bomb went through the roof of the school, and continued down to the ground floor, where it exploded in the Infants Class. Eighteen children were killed and many more injured.

23. St Mary's and St Joseph's Catholic Church was originally in Gates Street, built in 1856 and demolished by a land mine on 8 December 1940. The site is marked by a mound and crucifix in the school grounds. The present church, built in 1954 to the design of the architect Adrian Gilbert Scott, has Moorish influences.

24. Blessed John Roche School was built in 1951 on the site of the original church of St Mary and St Joseph. First called Cardinal Griffin School, it was amalgamated with St Victoire's (Howrah House) and renamed Philip Howard. The school later underwent a further name change, and reverted to being a boys' school.

St Mary's and St Joseph's Catholic Church, destroyed by a land mine, 1940.

● **Walk past the school down Canton Street to Saracen Street.**

25. Howrah House (site only), was built in 1790 by Duncan Dunbar, owner of Dunbar's Wharf. In 1881 it became the Convent of the Faithful Companions of Jesus, the first Reverend Mother being Madame Veronica Connolly. It was a girls' school until World War Two. The ruins were demolished in 1950 to create Saracen Street and build the blocks of flats occupying the site.

26. At 7–9 Stainsby Road, Luke House was built in 1933 to house the East London Nursing Society. It was founded in 1868 by Mrs Wigram, wife of the famous shipbuilder of Blackwall, and her daughters Harriet and Eliza worked for the society for over 40 years. It was the oldest nursing society in London and the second oldest in Britain. The nurses were amalgamated with the London Hospital in 1973, and the house is now a hostel for Queen Mary and Westfield College.

27. Poplar Hippodrome (site only), stood on the corner of Stainsby Road, although this part of the road has disappeared, and Canton Road curves round to meet the main road. Built as

Poplar Hippodrome, East India Dock Road.

the Prince's Theatre in 1905, by the 1920s it was a cinema. The Hippodrome was demolished in 1950 following bomb damage during the Blitz.

● **Walk back up East India Dock Road.**

28. St Stephen's Church (site only), built in 1867, was severely damaged in 1945 and its site is marked by the stone wall alongside the East India Dock Road.
29. The Green family vault is in a corner of the park, which was once the burial ground for the Congregational Chapel. George Green is buried here, as are his second wife Elizabeth and

Trinity Park, with 'The Dockers' sculpture in the foreground, Green's Almshouses to the left, Mayflower School on the right and St Mary's and St Joseph's Catholic Church in the distance.

their son Richard. There is also a sculpture of two figures, entitled 'The Dockers', created by Sydney Harpley in 1962.

30. Trinity Chapel, built by George Green, was opened on 5 August 1841. Completely demolished by bombs in August 1944, it was replaced by the present Trinity Church in 1951. The building, which combines the Methodist and Congregational churches, is listed. The architects were C.C. Handisyde and D.R. Stark.

31. The Queen Victoria Seamen's Rest has been on this site for almost 100 years. The Art Nouveau neo-Tudor building fronting Jeremiah Street, designed by architects Gunton and Gunton, was opened in 1902, on the site of the Magnet pub. Starting life in 1843 in the

Queen Victoria Seamen's Rest and Trinity Church, East India Dock Road.

Methodist Chapel in Cable Street, the Seamen's Mission moved to Commercial Road and then to its present site. The building suffered bomb damage during World War Two, and the new block fronting the East India Dock Road was opened in October 1953. The mission is a bed and breakfast hostel run entirely as a charity, and is home to many retired, unemployed and serving seamen.

32. Green's Home for Sailors, founded by George Green in 1841, was the first private sailors' home, built for the use of seamen who sailed in Green's ships. Following Richard Green's death, the building became the Board of Trade Offices, and has now been converted into residential flats.

33. No.153 East India Dock Road, Palm Cottage, is a charming Georgian-style house built for Thomas Ditchburn, shipbuilder of Blackwall. He built over 400 ships including Queen Victoria's favourite yacht, the *Fairy*, built in 1845.

A view down East India Dock Road of George Green School.

34. George Green School was built in 1828, one of the many schools set up by George Green in Poplar. Others were the Preston Road School in 1833, Trinity School in 1841 and Bow Lane School in 1847. The first school was on the corner of Chrisp Street, and was later moved to the site of Monastery House in 1884. In the 1960s a new George Green School was built near Island Gardens on the Isle of Dogs, and the present building houses a sixth-form centre.

● Continue along past Chrisp Street Market and turn into Ida Street and Lodore Street.

St Frideswide's door, carved by Alice Liddell of *Alice in Wonderland*.

35. St Frideswide's Church (site only) was on Lodore Street. In 1888 a Mission Church was founded in a cottage in Lodore Street by Christ Church College Oxford, and the building was consecrated in 1893. It had a beautiful wooden door carved by Alice Hargreaves, née Liddell, daughter of the Dean of Christ Church, who was immortalised by Lewis Carroll in *Alice in Wonderland*. The upper panel of the door depicted a scene in the life of the Saxon Princess St Frideswide. The church was destroyed in a bombing raid in 1945, and the door was removed to St Frideswide's Church in Osney, Oxford.

36. St Frideswide's Mission, Lodore Street was built in 1889 by Catherine Mary Phillimore, and opened by Mrs Gladstone, wife of the Prime Minister. Catherine Phillimore had her own rooms in the mission, which she shared with her companion Mary Hervey. They worked at the project until the outbreak of war in 1914. The entrance arch with the statue of St Frideswide survived into the 1990s but has now sadly been vandalised.

37. The Jerusalem Coffee House was opened in 1900 by Catherine Phillimore following a trip to the Holy Land. It became the Poplar Association for Befriending Servant Girls. Catherine's sister Lucy, who was Mrs Gladstone's private secretary from 1892 to 1900 was also involved with the Jerusalem Coffee House. Lucy became Vice President of the Society for the Propagation of the Gospel. Both sisters were published authors, and Catherine was a recognised authority on Dante and the Italian Renaissance.

The entrance to St Frideswide's Mission, Lodore Street.

- **Return to East India Dock Road via Ida Street and cross over the road.**

38. At the corner of Bazely Street at 11.50am on 7 March 1945 a V2 rocket demolished the Eagle public house and the premises of the Sisters of St John the Divine. Twenty people were killed in the attack, and a further 120 injured. Many of the victims had been waiting at the bus stop in front of All Saints' Church. Two days later, on Wednesday 9 May, the Royal Family paid a visit to the scene, as part of their tour of the East End bomb sites.

- **Return to All Saints' Docklands Station or the bus stop on East India Dock Road.**

The Jerusalem Coffee House, Follett Street.

Walk 4
Blackwall and the East India Docks

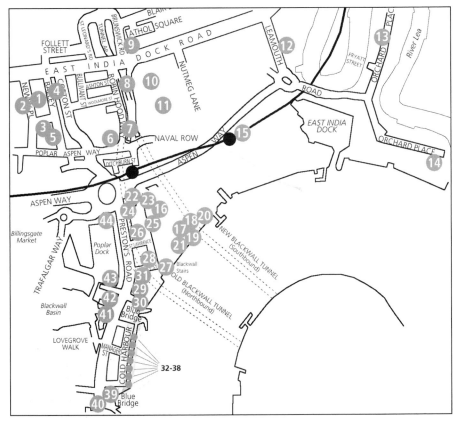

Travel to All Saints' Station on the Docklands Light Railway. Exit eastwards toward All Saints' Church, OR travel from Mile End underground station on the D6 bus route to the All Saints' stop.

1. All Saints' Parish Church in Newby Place was built after the inhabitants of Poplar made a petition to Parliament in 1816. Until then Poplar formed part of the parish of Stepney, with

St Dunstan's the mother church. The church, consecrated in 1823, was designed by Charles Hollis and built by Thomas Morris of Blackwall on land gifted by Mrs Ann Newby. George Green of Blackwall Yard provided the money in the form of a loan, which was later taken on by the West India Dock Company.

2.   All Saints' Rectory was also built on Mrs Newby's land. She had gifted her house for use as the rectory, but it was demolished and a grand new house was built for the rector on the site. For years peacocks roamed the gardens and the décor of the house reflects this theme.

3.   Montague Place, a row of elegant early 19th-century houses, of different sizes and frontages, with some interesting wrought-iron balconies, stands behind the church. The street is named after James Montague, who was a Poplar churchwarden from 1804 to 1817.

4.   No.1 Bow Lane, now Bazely Street, was the site of the East London branch of the Nursing Sisters of St John the Divine, set up in 1880 by Julia Childers and Julia Lake. The sisters first came to Poplar in 1866 during a cholera epidemic. They lost everything when their nursing home was demolished during a V2 attack on 7 March 1945. The street is named after Revd Thomas Bazely, who was rector of Poplar from 1839 to 1860.

5.   Hester Hawes Almshouses (site only) for poor widows stood next door to the Greenwich Pensioner. Built from a legacy given by Hester Hawes, a resident of Woodstock Terrace, who died in 1696, the cottages were single rooms, three on either side of a small courtyard. An archway led into Bow Lane, now Bazely Street. The cottages were in use until 1940. The Greenwich Pensioner pub dates from 1827, and replaced another tavern on the site.

● Walk down Poplar High Street to Robin Hood Gardens.

6.   The Queen's Theatre (site only) was situated at the top end of Poplar High Street, on the north side. Many famous music hall stars and other entertainers began their careers here. Gracie Fields was an unknown when she sang at the Queen's. Other entertainers include Gertie Gitana, Betty Driver, Nellie Wallace, Kate Carney and Vesta Victoria.

7.   The Blackwall Tunnel was opened on 22 May 1897. The Prince of Wales, later Edward VII, and Princess Alexandra rode through in their royal carriage from Poplar to Greenwich. The

The East India Dock gate and Blackwall Tunnel entrance.

tunnel took five years to build and 600 men were employed in its construction. Nine men lost their lives through various accidents. The tunnel measures 4,460 feet long, of which 1,220 feet is under the River Thames. The original archway on the Blackwall side was demolished when the second tunnel was constructed, completed in 1967, but an identical one can been seen on the Greenwich side, which has survived.

8. The East India Dock gates and Tunnel Gardens (site only) were alongside the tunnel. The commemorative stone which marked the place of the massive dock gates, which were demolished in 1912 and rebuilt further back, only to be pulled down during the construction of the second Blackwall tunnel between 1963 and 1967, was once again removed and replaced on a rebuilt section of the wall, a bit further back from the original spot. The elegant plaque commemorating the opening of the tunnel can be found on the wall of the underpass, by the bus stop.

Poplar Hospital, East India Dock Road.

9. Poplar Hospital (site only) was sited opposite the East India Dock gates, on the corner of Quag Lane (Brunswick Road) and the East India Dock Road. It was opened in July 1855 as a hospital for accidents and emergencies in what was formerly the Custom House of the East India Company. The founders were Richard and Henry Green, J.D.A. Samuda and Charles Mayer. In-patient treatment was strictly for males. Poplar Hospital suffered severe damage during the Blitz and was demolished in the 1970s, leaving only a chimney standing.

● **Walk back to Naval Row.**

10. The East India Docks were built shortly after the West India Docks. East Indiamen returning home laden with cargo and goods from the Indies came up the river to Blackwall, where they discharged their cargoes into decked lighters, or hoys, to be taken by road to London. However,

East India Docks: a panoramic view with the Lea on the left and Blackwall Reach and Blackwall Point in the centre, and the Isle of Dogs on the right.

pilferage from merchant ships in the Pool of London led to large losses and a Bill was presented to Parliament in 1799 for the construction of enclosed docks on the Isle of Dogs. The West India Docks were completed in 1803 and the East India Company then acquired the Brunswick Basin in 1806, which became the East India Export Dock. The Import Dock was constructed north-east of the Brunswick Basin, the engineer in charge of this project being Ralph Walker. The section of dock wall in Naval Row is all that remains of the massive wall enclosing the East India Import Dock.

11. The East India Import Dock was one of the sites chosen for building the Phoenix units of the floating Mulberry harbour used for the D-Day landings. The dock was later filled in, and a new development by the Nordic Construction Company, Mulberry Place, now occupies the site. The Financial Times printing offices occupied a large building alongside the East India Dock Road, but they have moved on. Tower Hamlets Town Hall is situated in Mulberry Place.

12. Pepper and spice warehouses were built by the East India Company in Leamouth Road. The gateway had an interesting relief in coade stone of a staff and entwined serpents, the symbol of healing, which could refer to the spices stored

MOWLEM – TAYLOR WOODROW
STRICTLY NO ADMITTANCE
TO THE GENERAL PUBLIC

The ruins of the Spice Warehouse entrance.

in the warehouses. During the development of the area, the gateposts were demolished and replaced with a crude replica.

13. The Orchard, as it has been known for centuries, is where the River Lea curves upon itself before opening into the Thames. In 1595 John Churchman, a merchant tailor, owned a couple of orchards here, and a map from around 1619 shows the orchard and a house surrounded by a moat. Orchard House was later used by the East India Company to billet their lascars or Asian sailors, then taken over by a glass manufacturer. Glassmaking was an important industry until 1875, employing about 75% of the inhabitants of the area, who were nearly all related. Plate glass was made there and sent all over the country, including all the glass used in the making of the Crystal Palace, but in around 1875 competition from the US glass industry ruined the Orchard House glass factory and caused it to close down. Many glassworkers emigrated to New Albany, Indiana, in America.

14. The Trinity House workshops and lighthouse are situated at the mouth of the River Lea. Trinity House was founded in 1514 by Henry VIII, and later based at Deptford in 1745. They started leasing land at Blackwall in 1803 and by 1875 had extended to an acre. The small octagonal lighthouse was built in around 1860. It had no navigational function but was used to train lighthouse keepers in the art of maintaining lanterns. The warehouse served as a weather station for the Metereological Office, and Michael Faraday, who was scientific adviser to Trinity House, carried out his experiments in this building. In 1988 Trinity House transferred all of its repair and maintenance work from Blackwall to Harwich.

15. East India or Brunswick Docklands Station offers an excellent view of Brunswick Pier and the site of the East India Dock Export Basin, now filled in by Barratts for their new housing scheme.

16. Green and Perry's Dockyard (site only) was known to sailors all over the world. George Green was apprenticed to John Perry at Perry's Yard in 1782. In 1796, aged 29, he married Sarah Perry and went into partnership with her father, and in 1803 he also became a partner

Perry's Masthouse and a panoramic view of Blackwall Yard.

with John and Philip Perry, the sons, and John and William Wells. The senior John Perry, a widower, had married Mary Green, George Green's sister. The shipbuilding firm became Perry, Sons and Green. John Perry died in 1810, and Perry's Yard became Green's Yard as George Green and his sons Richard and Henry took control of shipbuilding at Blackwall. The Greens lived in a large house in the middle of the yard, which had originally been built by Henry Johnson, then rebuilt and enlarged to accommodate George's growing family. In 1837 George Green built the first Blackwall frigate, the famous *Seringapatam* and, for the next 30 years, the Blackwall frigates dominated passenger trade. Robert Wigram entered into partnership with Richard Green, but in 1843 a split occurred between the two shipping magnates and the yard was divided. Wigram sold part of his site to the Midland Railway, and Blackwall dock was filled in to provide a railway depot. The Greens built another dock alongside and continued to build and repair ships.

17. Blackwall Railway Station was constructed alongside Brunswick Wharf and opened for business in July 1840. It was the terminus for the London and Blackwall Railway, built by Robert Stephenson and George Parker Bidder. Referred to as the 'fourpenny rope', the railway was operated by means of a pulley and ropes. Two sets of carriages operated in opposite directions, and the ropes were worked from either end by stationary steam-engines, used alternately for up and down trains. The reason for this curious invention was the fear that the sparks from a conventional engine driven by coal would accidentally set light to cargo lying at the docks. Blackwall Railway Station closed in 1926. In the 1980s the

The Blackwall Railway Terminus, Brunswick Pier.

line was refurbished and the Docklands Light Railway, with its distinctive blue and red carriages, began operating in 1987. The line now runs from Bank and Fenchurch Street to Blackwall and Beckton.

18. The Brunswick Tap, built in 1845 as a hotel, was intended to cater for railway passengers. The Tap was later converted into the dock master's house.

19. The Virginia Settlers Memorial was unveiled on 30 June 1928, a gift from the Association for the Preservation of Virginia Antiquities, which presented a bronze plaque commemorating the Virginia Settlers, the first permanent English settlers in America, which was placed on the dock master's house. The house was severely damaged during the Blitz, and the plaque was removed. In 1951 a new memorial was constructed of granite and stone from the old West India Dock Gate, with a bronze mermaid by sculptor Harold Brown. Blackwall Station and the dock master's house were demolished during the construction of the Brunswick power station in 1958 and the bronze statue and plaque disappeared. In 1971 the granite memorial was removed to Brunswick Pier and a new plaque was placed on it. When the Brunswick power station was demolished in 1989 the plaque was removed. Following the regeneration of the area, now called Virginia Quay, Barratt Homes has refurbished the memorial, which is now embellished with an astrolabe and new plaque, and the granite monument is mounted on a large plinth.

20. Brunswick Wharf was built in 1832 by the East India Dock Company as a steam wharf for paddle steamers. The engineer for the project was George Parker Bidder. The Brunswick Wharf was built of cast iron sheet piling, which was not only a great saving in cost, but also the first major application of the system.

● Walking eastwards toward Reuters' Headquarters, and the site of the Brunswick Tavern brings us to the Meridian Line.

21. The Brunswick Tavern (site only) was situated at the western end of the wharf. The tavern was built by William Cubitt for the East India Dock Company to the design of Ralph Walker. A three-storey building of yellow brick with large bay windows, curved balconies and a terrace on the first floor, it had a magnificent bay window which ran the length of the building overlooking the Thames, and it stood precisely on the meridian line. Samuel Lovegrove, who already owned the West India Dock Tavern in Coldharbour, the Crown and Sceptre at Greenwich and the Coffee House at Ludgate Hill, took over the lease. The Brunswick became the fashionable haunt of society people, who came from London to enjoy their whitebait dinners with champagne. The popularity of the Brunswick lasted until the 1860s when the rendezvous for fashionable diners shifted to Greenwich. The Ship, the Crown and Sceptre (owned by Lovegrove) and the Trafalgar took over from the Brunswick.

A philanthropic society headed by Lord Radstock bought the Brunswick and ran it as an Emigrants Home. Families awaiting passage to Australia during the gold rush years waited here. In 1851 the Canterbury Association, headed by Lord Lyttelton, established a colony in New Zealand for emigrants from East London and about 1,800 people were despatched in a total of 10 ships. When the Queensland Government withdrew its support of emigrants, however, numbers fell drastically, and by 1895, the Emigrants Home was

The Brunswick Tavern in 1926, shortly before it was demolished.

forced to close. Until the outbreak of World War One it was used as a convalescent home for children, and it later became the offices of Messrs R. & H. Green and Silley Weir Ltd, shipbuilders and repairers at the adjacent Blackwall Yard. In September 1930 demolition workers moved in and the Brunswick was razed to the ground.

22. The Accumulator Tower was built by the Midland Railway Company in 1881 to provide hydraulic power for the company's new dock and warehouses. It is now a wine warehouse.

23. Charrington Gardner and Locker's oil depot at Blackwall was opened in 1959 on the site of the old Blackwall docks. The depot closed in 1987 and was left derelict for a number of years. It is now being developed.

24. The Marshal Keate pub (site only) was situated in Prestons Road, but unfortunately did not survive the sweeping changes that took place in Blackwall in the 1980s. The pub gets its first mention in the rate books in 1843, when the landlord was James Sadd. There appeared to have been three sections to the pub, the Marshal Keate Hotel, Union Dock Hotel and the Railway Tavern. In 1905 the premises were offered for sale by the Midland Railway Company, which had purchased them in 1881.

25. Blackwall Way led to Blackwall Stairs. As early as 1553 it was recorded that Poplar and Blackwall had seven alehouses. During the 18th and 19th centuries, with the increase in activity along the river at Blackwall, travellers and inhabitants had a choice of at least 15 inns or taverns. The Globe, Old Hob, Shoulder of Mutton and Pig, and the Ship all stood

on the east side of the Causeway. The Brunswick Arms (Coopers Arms), White Swan and the George stood on the west side. There were five more on the riverbank between Blackwall Stairs and Globe Stairs: The King's Arms, the India Arms, the Britannia, the Plough and the Artichoke. In Coldharbour could be found the West India Dock Tavern, the Fishing Smack and the Gun.

26. The Canada Estate consisted of six blocks of flats built between Blackwall Way and Prestons Road. Some of the buildings were damaged during the Blitz and later demolished, but the row of cottages in St Lawrence Street survived.

27. Blackwall Stairs were at the southernmost end of Blackwall Way from where most early travellers would have embarked for their journeys. On 19 December 1606, three ships, the

Blackwall Stairs, with the White Swan in the background.

Susan Constant, under the command of Christopher Newport, the *God Speed*, captained by Bartholomew Gosnold, and the *Discovery* captained by John Ratcliffe, set sail from Blackwall for Virginia, carrying 105 men, the first permanent English settlers in America. The leader of the expedition was John Smith.

28. The White Swan pub in Yabsley Street is a fairly modern building, although from excavations at the rear of the pub there is evidence that a much older building or buildings stood on this site.

29. Walter Raleigh's house (site only) was situated in Raleana Way. The waste recycling plant replaces Northumberland Wharf, which in turn was built on part of Coldharbour, which joined the Causeway. There is no trace of St Nicholas's Church, or even of Raleana Way, in

The house in Coldharbour said to have belonged to Sir Walter Raleigh.

which stood a two-storey house referred to locally as Sir Walter Raleigh's house. It was demolished during the construction of the first Blackwall Tunnel, completed in 1897. The mushroom-shaped ventilation shaft indicates the position of the tunnel, and there is a corresponding shaft on the south side of the river.

30. The Artichoke Tavern (site only) was certainly in existence in 1754, when Peter Lord, the landlord, advertised the opening of the Long Room, 'a fine place for seeing ships launched'. In 1765 the advertisement read: 'Peter Lord at the Artichoke Tavern at Blackwall thinks it his duty to acquaint the public, that the much-admired fish, called white bait, are now just come in, and are in great perfection.' The Artichoke Tavern was still serving whitebait in 1841, when the landlords were Brendel and Roberts.

31. St Nicholas's Church, Blackwall (site only) was built following the construction of the Canada Estate, for the new community. The site acquired was the one where Raleigh's house originally stood. A Miss Trevor donated £4,000 to the building fund and the church opened in 1900. Built entirely of red brick and measuring 65ft by 35ft by 50ft high, St Nicholas's was lit by electricity and was the first building in Poplar to have such lighting. The church was

The vicar and members of the congregation of St Nicholas's Church, Blackwall Stairs.

badly damaged during the Blitz, and was used as a waste disposal centre during World War Two.

32. Coldharbour ran along the bank of the river, with houses on one side only. Daniell's view of Coldharbour shows a row of fine houses along this part of the river, but it was painted before these early 19th-century houses were built, after the construction of the West India Docks in 1802.

Dockmaster's House, No.1 Coldharbour.

33. No.1 Coldharbour, Isle House, was built in 1825 and was formerly the dock master's residence, designed by the architect Sir John Rennie.

34. No.3 Coldharbour, Nelson House, was remodelled in 1820 by joining two existing houses. Samuel Grainger, a coal merchant, was responsible for this refurbishment, and the façade of the house shows the unequal width of the two original buildings. The house is so called because Nelson was reputed to have stayed there. Nelson did visit Blackwall, when his ship, on which he won the Battle of Aboukir, was being built there, and probably did indeed stay in Coldharbour.

35. Nos 5 and 7 Coldharbour were built in 1808–09 and retain many of their original features. There are four floors in each house, each floor having a front and back room, with a centre stair and landing area.

Nelson House in Coldharbour.

Nos 9–13 were built in 1971 by the GLC and they partly replaced a late Victorian public house. No.15 is an early Victorian house built in 1845 by Benjamen Bluett, a local mastmaker, and originally contained his workshop as well as living accommodation.

36. Old Wharf site. The windows on the south side of No.15 overlook the former Metropolitan Asylum Board's ambulance station, known as North Wharf, recently demolished. From 1885 onwards smallpox patients were ferried out to floating isolation hospitals moored in the Thames. The iron-clad river wall was erected in around 1860 by the General Steam Navigation Company, which imported live cattle for slaughter. This practice ended in the 1870s. The wall is constructed of concrete overlaid with five rows of large overlapping iron plates rivetted together. Each plate measures 8ft by 2ft 6in.

37. No.19 Coldharbour, the old Thames police station, was built in 1893–4 to accommodate the Thames police, whose previous HQ had been afloat on a ship called *The Royalist*. It is one of only two permanent river police stations ever built on the Thames, the other being in Wapping. Designed by John Butler, architect and surveyor to the Metropolitan Police, the horizontal bands of brick and stone show the influence of the New Scotland Yard building, which Butler helped to design.

38. The Gun public house is the only surviving riverside tavern in Blackwall. There was a public house here in 1716 called the King and Queen, which later became the Rose and Crown, and then the Ramsgate Pink. The pub became the Gun in 1770. The interior has an interesting concealed staircase with a Napoleonic spy hole facing out to the river, which was used to

The Gun public house in Coldharbour.

check that the coast was clear of revenue men. A room above the bar is called the Lady Hamilton Room, and the pub is reputed to be haunted. The pub was rumoured to be connected by a secret passage to No.3 Coldharbour.

39. The dock cottages originally numbered 29–51. However, 50 and 51 were demolished in 1993 when Prestons Road was being widened yet again. The cottages were erected in 1889-90 by William Warren, an estate agent in East India Dock Road, and George Larman, a builder from Plaistow. They are built on land that belonged to the East and West India Dock Company.

40. The Blue Bridge is the sixth bridge over the eastern entrance to the South Dock (West India Docks). It was erected in 1967–9 and spans 110ft. It was quite common for commuters to be caught by 'a bridger', when all traffic came to a halt to let ships pass into or out of the docks.

● **Walk back along the east side of Prestons Road, past Lovegrove Walk, named after the landlord of the Brunswick at Blackwall. There is an interesting fountain here.**

41. There was an iron swing bridge over the old entrance to Poplar Dock and the Blackwall Basin, which disappeared during the widening of Prestons Road in 1989.

42. Bridge House, built in 1819–20, was designed by John Rennie for the principal dockmaster of the West India Dock Company. It became the offices of the PLA Police in 1954.

43. Poplar Dock was first developed in 1827–9, and the project engineer was Sir John Rennie. In 1850 it was converted by the East and West India Dock Companies and the Birmingham Junction Railway Company, later the North London Line, to form a railway dock for colliers. All the warehouses were destroyed in the Blitz.

44. Billingsgate Market, with its distinctive architecture, can be seen from here. This world-famous fish market moved from its tradional centuries-old site in Lower Thames Street to Docklands in January 1982.

A view of Canary Wharf from the old dock entrance, Prestons Road, 1993.

● **Return to Poplar High Street and Newby Place, back to All Saints' Station.**

Walk 5
Bromley St Leonard

The parish of Bromley St Leonard covered an area of approximately 475 acres. It was situated along the east boundary of the London Borough of Tower Hamlets and extended along a north-south axis, immediately west of the River Lea, for a distance of about one and a quarter miles, south of the Bow Bridge road intersection.

Brambeley, as the district was then known, was important because of its position on the River Lea, whose waters were harnessed to power the mills in the area. It consisted of the Upper Manor and the Lower Manor. The Upper Manor of Bromley St Leonard possessed a rich historical past extending over 1,000 years. Many buildings of outstanding interest, which were a visible link with the past, existed until the 1930s, but most were demolished during the county council's clearance programme or destroyed later during the Blitz. Further historical links were eradicated in 1969 by the county council's road proposals for the northern approach road to the Blackwall Tunnel, which involved the cutting of an underpass at the nearby Bow Bridge intersection. This completely removed the blitzed remains of the parish church of St Mary and St Leonard, together with a substantial portion of the churchyard, which contained many Huguenot tombs. Originally Bromley was described as the parish of Bromley St Leonard, which refers to the priory and convent at Stratford-atte-Bow, which meant 'Stratford by the bridge'. It was referred to simply as Bromley, until the confusion with Bromley in Kent caused the postal authorities to call it Bromley-by-Bow.

The priory was probably in existence during the time of William the Conqueror, and consisted of a prioress and nuns of the Benedictine order. By the end of the 16th century, the nunnery buildings, with the exception of the chapel and priory house, were demolished and the property that had belonged to the priory subsequently became the Upper Manor of Bromley.

The old church, which was originally the chancel or chapel of the Convent of St Leonard, was demolished in 1842, many of the ancient monuments being incorporated in the new building. Sadly, the church was severely damaged during World War Two and was completely demolished to allow the northern approach to the Blackwall Tunnel to be constructed. Only a small part of the churchyard, in a very dilapidated state, has survived.

Bromley-by-Bow was one of the few areas in Tower Hamlets to retain its rural aspect long after so much of the East End comprised factories, manufactories and poorly built houses catering for the working classes. Bromley village had its village green, situated opposite the church of St Leonard. Along High Street Bromley were the usual row of shops and houses, including the blacksmith's shop. The green had stocks, a whipping post and a ducking stool.

James Dunstan, clerk of the Bromley Vestry for 30 years, records in 1862 that the stocks were set up in front of a house at the north corner of the entrance to Back Alley, but had by then been removed. Back Alley was renamed Botolph Passage. In this vicinity too was the bowling green, on the west side of Devons Lane (Road). The site was later used for market gardens.

Robert Owen was appointed churchwarden of Bromley St Leonard's in 1663, an office held for a year, when he was landlord of the Ship Tavern. Four Mill Street was renamed St Leonard's Street, and the Ship must have been situated somewhere between the church and the Four Mills, near Coventry Cross.

Some of the entries in the churchwarden's accounts give a graphic picture of life in rural Bromley. For instance, in May 1681, a man was found dead in 'ye old Barne over against the Wheelwrights by ye Red Cow' a description that might apply to a village in the heart of the countryside.

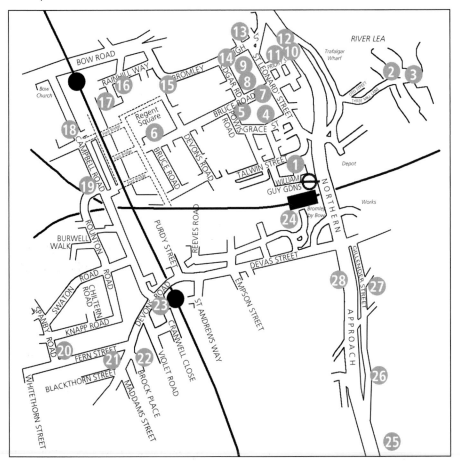

Before the dissolution of the monasteries the Manor of Bromley Hall was in the possession of the Priory of Christchurch (Holy Trinity), Aldgate, but when the priory was dissolved in 1531 the property passed into the hands of the Crown. Around the middle of the 16th century the manor was held by Ralph Sadler, but the property changed hands frequently. William Ferrers probably built Bromley Hall as his manor house shortly after acquiring the manor in 1616.

By the 18th century Bromley Hall was being used as a calico printing factory. In 1799 the property was sold to Joseph Foster of Bromley, a calico printer. Through the 18th and 19th centuries Bromley Hall and its surrounding buildings were used as factories of various kinds.

The Regions Beyond Missionary Union, whose headquarters were at Harley House in the Bow Road, occupied the hall from 1894 to 1914. The premises were then taken over by the Royal College of St Katharine, together with 228 Brunswick Road as an annexe, and used as an infant welfare centre.

Bromley Hall and the adjoining premises were damaged during World War Two, and in 1949 the Royal Foundation put Bromley Hall up for sale, together with the site of No.240. In 1951 the London County Council put a preservation order on Bromley Hall, and the building is still standing, now used by a garage.

The area named Bow Common in the middle of the last century was, in fact, part of Bromley parish. At one time a large expanse of uncultivated, unhedged land, in the 19th century it became the site of chemical and other factories, giving off noxious smells. A new canal was excavated from the Lea at Bromley to Limehouse, known as the Limehouse Cut. Railway development in particular changed the rural aspect of the parish, and by 1850 the last of the farmhouses and homesteads of old Bromley had gone. Within the space of 50 years the population had increased from 4,000 to 24,000. With realignments of the major roads within the area the last of the village of Bromley-by-Bow has been swept away.

Bromley St Leonard Walk

This walk starts at Bromley-by-Bow underground station. Exit left, and walk down the slope toward St Leonard's Street. Almost immediately on the left can be seen:

1. William Guy Gardens is a development of council houses on the approximate site of Bromley Workhouse.

● **Follow the right-hand pavement along the Blackwall Tunnel Northern Approach and go through the underpass toward the Tesco superstore. Continue along Three Mills Lane, and cross the small bridge over the Lea.**

2. The River Lea flows from its source in Bedfordshire to join the Thames at Bow Creek. Traditionally, it marks the boundary between Middlesex and Essex. Near the Temple Mills on Hackney Marshes, the Lea branches out into several tributaries. South-west of these is the Lea Navigation. Two of the streams, known as Three Mills back river and Three Mills Wall river, as well as the main river, flow down to Three Mills, where they are joined by the Abbey mill stream. The River Lea and all its branches are tidal almost as far as Temple Mills. Originally there were six tidal corn mills, described at the beginning of the 20th century as 'the most remarkable group of mills in Essex'. Of these only Three Mills still exists.

'Beating the Bounds' on the River Lea at Bromley-by-Bow, c.1882. The Revd George How, Vicar of St Leonard's, officiates.

3. Three Mills is often referred to as being within Bromley but is in fact situated within the parish of West Ham, now part of Newham. The House Mill and the Clock Mill are the last remaining tide mills in the London area. The third mill was demolished during the reign of Edward VI to improve navigation along the River Lea. Over the centuries the mills changed

Three Mills at Bromley-by-Bow.

hands several times. Daniel Bisson and his son owned the mills by 1751 and in 1776 the House Mill was rebuilt and the Clock Mill was rebuilt in 1817 by Philip Metcalfe. The House Mill ceased operating in 1941 and the Clock Mill closed in 1952. By 1872 the distilling business seems to have gone into decline, and by 1893 the property was transferred to J. & W. Nicholson. Damaged during World War Two, the buildings were later converted into bonded warehouses. In 1995 the Millers House was restored by English Heritage and the mills are now managed as a heritage site.

● **Return to the Bromley-by-Bow side of the Northern Approach and walk through the estate back into St Leonards Street.**

The War Memorial in Bromley   Archway in the park.
Recreation Park.

4. Bromley Recreation Ground was laid out by the London County Council in 1900. This was the site of Tudor House, an early 17th-century house with a large garden. The last occupier was George Gammon Rutty, a local builder and highways contractor. He embellished the garden with an archway which came from the inner courtyard of Northumberland House, Charing Cross, a 17th-century building demolished in 1874. There were also two stone statues and a ship's figurehead as part of this display. Part of the Park was acquired for a health centre in 1995, and the park has been embellished with some interesting stone sculptures.

● **Continue walking down Grace Street and turn into Powis Road.**

5. Kingsley Hall, Powis Road was built by Muriel and Doris Lester, two sisters from Loughton in Essex, who began their charitable work in Bow before World War One. They rented No.60 Bruce Road and started a nursery school, and in 1912 were joined by their brother Kingsley. Two years later Kingsley died, aged 26. The sisters then bought an old chapel, the Zion Chapel on the corner of Botolph Road and Eagling Road, and began their settlement work. The present building was erected in 1928, the architect being C. Cowles-Voysey, and was named Kingsley Hall in memory of their brother. Mahatma Gandhi stayed here for six weeks during 1931 when he attended the Round Table Conference at St James's Palace, during the negotiations for Indian independence. After World War Two the building was used by a Dr Laing as a psychiatric unit, during which time the patients destroyed a great deal of the interior. Doris Lester died in 1965 and Muriel Lester in 1968. After years of neglect Kingsley Hall was restored and is now run as a community centre.

Kingsley Hall in Powis Road, with the Gandhi memorial plaque.

- **Walk toward Bruce Road and turn left, and then continue to the corner of the road.**

6. The Children's Nursery on Bruce Road was built by Muriel and Doris Lester in 1923, on the site of an old stable on the corner of Eagling Road and Bruce Road. It was opened by H.G. Wells, the author, who was guest of honour. There is an interesting mural inside by the artist

and writer, Eve Garnett, showing children from the slums in the East End walking through a door into the countryside. Unfortunately, an insensitive electrical engineer has positioned the red wiring for the fire alarm right across it.

● **Return along Bruce Road, continue along the road. On the right is the Old Palace School, and on the left is:**

7. Bromley-by-Bow Congregational Church and community centre, built in the 1860s, was destroyed in an air raid in 1940, but was rebuilt and reopened for worship on 15 March 1958. It is now a community centre, combining arts and crafts and care in the community. The Revd Andrew Mawson was the driving force behind the new £4 million health centre in the park to the rear.

8. The Old Palace, St Leonards Street (site only) was the second building of major importance in Bromley apart from the priory. Built in 1606, it was traditionally supposed to have been a hunting lodge built by James I. His arms, motto, crest and initials featured prominently in the state room. The house was altered in 1750, when it was converted into two dwellings. It later became a boarding school known as Palace House School. In 1893 the property was acquired by the School Board for London, for a new school building. Its demolition was the cause of a public protest, headed by the architect C.R. Ashbee. Desperate efforts were made to save some of the priceless fittings and artefacts. Eventually, the mantelpiece of the state room, together with the panelling and ceiling, a stone chimney-piece and other features were removed to the Victoria and Albert Museum, and displayed as the Bromley Room. Old Palace School now stands on the site.

9. A memorial plaque to the firemen killed during World War Two can be found on the wall of the Old Palace School. The school was used as a sub-station for the London Fire Brigade and as the HQ of the local rescue services. On the night of Saturday 19 April 1941, London and the East End saw some of the heaviest bombing raids, as over 1,026 tons of high explosive and 153,096 incendiary bombs rained down. Four fire service crews from Beckenham were directed to report to Old Palace School. Shortly before 2am the school received a direct hit, partially demolishing the building. Thirty-six firemen were killed, including all four of the Beckenham crews.

● **Walk toward Bromley High Street. On the right is Priory Street.**

10. The Benedictine priory (site only) was dedicated to St Leonard and was founded by William, Bishop of London, for a prioress and nine nuns. It was probably in existence from the time of William the Conqueror. Geoffrey Chaucer refers to the priory in his *Canterbury Tales*, when he describes one of the pilgrims, a prioress: 'French she spake full fair and fetisley (exquisitely)/ After the school of Stratford-atte-Bow/ For French of Paris was to her unknown'. Henry VIII gave the confiscated priory and land to Sir Ralph Sadler, who converted it into a country mansion. In 1635 the then Lord of the Manor, Sir John Jacob, demolished the converted priory buildings and erected a new manor house on the site. This was the Upper Manor of Bromley.

11. Bromley Manor House (site only) stood a little east of St Leonard's Street, between the churchyard and Priory Street. By the end of the 18th century it was a private boarding school for boys, Bromley School or Bromley Manor House Academy. The building was demolished early in the 19th century.

12. The church of St Mary with St Leonard (site only) was originally the lady chapel of the priory, which after being rebuilt in 1843 became the parish church for Bromley-by-Bow. Remains of Norman architecture existed within in the church: in the west wall were remains of a large arch ornamented with the lozenge and other Saxon mouldings. The church was bombed during the Blitz and the decision to widen the main road sealed its fate. The parish was then merged with St Mary's Bow. A memorial gate, of which only the stone archway

The How memorial gateway, St Leonard's churchyard.

remains, was erected in 1894, in memory of the Revd G.A. How, who served as vicar during the period 1872–93. The churchyard was closed for burials on 1 January 1856. The construction of the underpass caused the removal in 1969 of many graves; the remains were re-interred in the East London cemetery in Plaistow.

13. Tudor Lodge was the vicarage and church hall, and is the only surviving link with the past.

14. The Seven Stars Pub in Bromley High Street, on the corner of Bromley High Street and St Leonard's Street, now a private dwelling, was known in the 1980s as the Pearly Kings and Queens. It is a 19th-century construction, which replaced the original 17th-century Seven Stars, seen in early prints of Bromley Broadway. This corner of Bromley remained truly rural until the 1850s. The Seven Stars public house is mentioned in the churchwarden's account for 1681.

- **Continue walking up Bromley High Street toward the corner.**

15. Bromley High Street and Devon's Road formed a junction here, until the roads were realigned. In the central island was a drinking fountain with gas lamp and horse trough, referred to both by Sylvia Pankhurst and George Lansbury as the 'Obelisk'. This area was also the village green and had stocks and a whipping post until the mid-19th century. The Black Swan pub stood on the eastern side of the junction of High Street with Bow Road, and the Rose and Crown pub in Stroudley Walk (previously Devon's Road) was a 19th-century building which replaced the Bowling Green Inn that stood on one corner of the village bowling green.

16. St Agnes's School, Rainhill Way, was a Catholic primary school originally set up in Arrow Road by the Dominican sisters who lived at St Catherine's Convent. Later a new school was built in Botolph Road. The sisters left Bow in 1923 and the school was then taken over by the Sisters of the Sacred Hearts of Jesus and Mary, Chigwell. During World War Two the school was evacuated first to Oxford and then to Somerset. Following the war the children had classes in the top floor of Wellington Way School. In 1951 the new St Agnes's School opened on the present site.

17. The Drapers Almshouses in Priscilla Road, a delightful row of houses, are tucked away in a corner of Bromley-by-Bow. The almshouses were erected in 1706 for 12 poor persons, and an additional four houses were erected in 1836. Formerly the almshouses covered three sides of a quadrangle. There were six houses on each of the east and west sides and, at the southern end, facing the road, a central block comprising a central chapel with two houses either side. This block is the only remaining portion of the original almshouses. After being neglected for several years by the London County Council, which owned the buildings, they have since been refurbished and sold as private houses.

- **Follow Rainhill Way around and take the footbridge over the Docklands Railway line into Campbell Road**

18. No.26 Campbell Road was the home of Revd William and Mrs Mary Ann (Minnie) Lax, who lived here for 25 years. The Revd Lax was famous for his ministry at the Methodist Church in East India Dock Road. Minnie Lax worked for over 40 years with the Methodist Mission at Poplar. She led the sisterhood, which numbered 1,200 and was the largest in the country. Minnie was a familiar figure at the East India Dock gates, where she played her harmonium and sang hymns, attracting the crowds to hear her husband preach.

- **Walk down Campbell Road to the turning on the right, which is Rounton Road. There is a plaque here to Jack Warner, 'Dixon of Dock Green'.**

19. No.1 Rounton Road, in a turning off Campbell Road, was the home of the Waters family. Doris and Elsie Waters created the characters Gert and Daisy, and were stars of radio comedy from 1927. Born in Bow, where their father had a factory, they lived at No.1a with their brothers. Both the sisters were accomplished musicians, and formed the Bijou

Orchestra with their four brothers. Doris and Elsie Waters wrote all their own scripts, including the music and lyrics, and had the distinction of never repeating their material. They were both awarded the OBE for their achievements, as was their brother, Horace John Waters, who took the stage name of Jack Warner, becoming famous with his character 'Dixon of Dock Green'.

- **Continue down Rounton Road, which will lead into Knapp Road, take the first left and then turn left again into Fern Street.**

20. The Fern Street Settlement was opened by Clara Grant, who became head teacher at the infants' school in Devon's Road in 1900, and moved into a house in Fern Street. Inspired by the work of Canon Barnett at Toynbee Hall, she helped children in her school by providing

Devon's Road School, now Clara Grant School.

A portrait of Clara Grant, founder of the Fern Street Settlement.

them with breakfast, decent clothes, boots, and even handkerchiefs. She collected toys, whistles, shells, beads, wooden reels, marbles, odd bits of wool and silk, patchwork scraps, old cards and cigarette cards. All these were sorted out and made into little bundles which were on sale every Saturday for a farthing. Clara Grant's 'farthing bundles' were in great demand, and the crowds grew unmanageable. She then devised a method of controlling the children. She built a small wooden arch on which the words were inscribed: 'Enter all ye children small, none can come who are too tall'. Still the crowds of children came. The Fern

Clara Grant, on the left, with her farthing bundles.

Street Settlement was bombed during the war, but was later rebuilt. Clara Grant died in October 1949, having been awarded the OBE a few months earlier. The wooden arch, her medal, and her picture can be seen at the Fern Street Settlement, which is now a community centre.

● **Walk down Fern Street, into Devon's Road.**

21. All Hallows Church, Bromley-by-Bow, was built in 1875, damaged during the Blitz, and then rebuilt. The present Archbishop of Canterbury, George Carey, was born in Fern Street and baptised in this church. There is also a memorial to Clara Grant within the church.

22. Glaucus Street (Brock Place) was the site of the ducking stool, which was kept repaired and in constant readiness for the punishment of 'profligate and troublesome women'. It stood in the middle of a large field on the south side of Devon's Lane. Ducking-pond Field, about halfway down Glaucus Street, was in use until the early 1800s. Nearby was a mound, a rubbish heap known as Boney, where children scavenged for scraps.

● **Continue walking up Devon's Road to its junction with Campbell Road.**

The Widows Son pub in Devon's Road.

23. The Widow's Son Pub, also known as the Bun House, is an established part of East End folk history. There was a pub on this site in 1810 called the Bun House, owned by a widow whose only son was lost at sea. Expecting him home for Easter, the widow had made some hot cross buns for him, and when he did not arrive, she hung the buns up on the rafters. Every year, she made a fresh batch of buns, hoping for his return. The tradition is still maintained in the pub, with the ceremony of the hanging of the buns on Good Friday being performed by a seaman. This annual ceremony is a condition in the lease.

● **Walk on up past the Devon's Road Docklands Station, and continue along to Devas Street.**

24. St Andrew's Hospital was opened in 1871 as the Poplar and Stepney Sick Asylum, for workhouse inmates requiring medical attention. The Bromley Workhouse was situated just behind the hospital. The site was acquired for £7,300 and the hospital was built at a cost of £43,000. The architects were Arthur and C. Harston of Poplar. St Andrew's is now part of Newham Health Authority.

● **Walk up to the Northern Approach and turn right. The construction of this highway swallowed up a great deal of what was the Lower Manor of Bromley, but even without crossing over the road (which is possible by an underpass a few hundred yards ahead) it is possible to view the remainder of the sites.**

25. Bromley Hall was the manor house of the Lower Manor of Bromley. During the reign of Richard I the manor was held by Ralph Triket, the king's Chamberlain. The Lower Manor belonged to the priory of Christchurch (Holy Trinity), Aldgate, but in 1531 the property passed into the hands of the Crown. The original manor house was demolished and William Ferrers probably built Bromley Hall shortly after acquiring the manor in 1616. The property changed hands through the years and Bromley Hall was used as factory premises. From 1894 to 1914 Bromley Hall was occupied by the Regions Beyond Missionary Union, whose headquarters were at Harley House in the Bow Road. In 1914, it was taken over by the Royal

St Katharine's Maternity Hospital, Brunswick Road, with the Poplar Library in the background.

College of St Katharine. Bromley Hall and the adjoining premises were damaged during World War Two and Nos 228, 230 and 240 were subsequently demolished. In 1951 the London County Council put a preservation order on Bromley Hall, and the building is still standing in Gillender Street, now used by a garage.

26. No.240 Brunswick Road (now on Gillender Street) came to be known misleadingly as the manor house, and many believed it to be the original manor house. It stood between the library and Bromley Hall and was built in around 1823. It was a large Georgian house with a frontage of about 80 feet. Perhaps the most famous of its occupants was William Samuel Woodin, the actor, who lived there from 1875 to 1888. He filled the house were a variety of old oak carvings, and covered the ceilings with paintings on canvas. On 20 October 1940 the house was badly damaged during a bombing raid and many of the wood carvings were destroyed. The building was subsequently demolished.

The Old Five Bells Temperance pub in St Leonard's Street.

27. Coventry Cross is a small area of Bromley occupied by large blocks of flats, but the name derived from the tavern which existed in 1690, when Coventry Cross was the scene of a parish dinner, part of the 'beating the bounds' ceremony. In 1660, 17s 10d was 'Layed out for the procession dinner'. Bills of the Overseers on these occasions showed such items as 'Paid for eating and drinking before dinner, fish, lobsters, anchovies, butter, capers, turnips, carrots, sweet sauce, pyes, cheese, fruit, punch, wine, brandy, tobacco, cakes for the boys, etc etc.' The practice of "beating the bounds" ceased over 100 years ago.

28. The Old Five Bells (site only) was a pub at 152 St Leonard's Street. In 1923 this old pub was taken over by the Temperance Society and converted into a 'dry' pub. It was opened amid great publicity by Ishbel MacDonald, daughter of the Prime Minister. It was run very successfully by Mrs Adams, wife of the Minister of Berger Hall, as a community and recreation centre until 1940. When the two Baptist churches were destroyed during the first nights of the Blitz in September 1940, the depleted congregation began to use the pub for their services. In 1945, Sister Esther Thynne, with the deaconesses from Berger Hall, converted the pub into the 'Poplar and Berger Baptist Tabernacle'. Sister Esther was the guiding light of the Tab and conducted services regularly, following the minister's retreat to the safety of Brighton. By 1949 work on a new church had begun, but Sister Esther did not live to see it. She died in November 1949 and her funeral was held in the Old Five Bells.

● **Return along the Northern Approach to the Bromley-by-Bow underground station.**

Walk 6
Bow and Bow Bridge

The hamlet of Bow originated from a settlement on the rising ground alongside the River Lea, and in the course of time the cluster of homesteads that arose formed a hamlet of the parish of Stepney.

The name Bow is said to be derived from the original bridge, built with a pronounced arch or bow, that was built over the River Lea at this site. The River Lea winds its way down to the Thames, with smaller streams and back rivers joining it along the way.

The great Roman military highway from London into Essex that led to Colchester, crossed the River Lea by a ford situated about a mile north of the Bow Bridge site. The ford was hazardous and, despite the fact that it may have been paved by the Romans, could not be easily crossed unless conditions were favourable. The area Old Ford takes its name from this Roman construction.

In around 1100 Queen Mathilda, the wife of King Henry I, while on her way to Barking Abbey, received a wetting while crossing the ford on horseback, and the accident resulted in the building of a bridge. This bridge naturally caused a diversion of the old traditional Roman road which followed what is now Old Ford Road, and in due course a more direct route was adopted, from Whitechapel to Bow, taking in the present Mile End Road. By 1655 the old Roman Road across Tower Hamlets had disappeared.

Queen Matilda provided for the upkeep and repair of the bridge, from income from manors and a water mill which she bought and placed in the care of the Abbess of Barking. The site of the water mill is now known as Abbey Mills. There is also some evidence that the original bridge had a chantry or chapel dedicated to St Catherine upon it. The bridge appears to have been rebuilt in the 14th century and probably again in 1741. However, the increasing traffic down the centuries caused considerable deterioration to the structure and by 1839, the bridge was rebuilt as a single oblate arch, known as a 'Pelly bridge'. By 1905 this too was in need of replacement and another bridge of iron girders, with two carriageways, replaced the 1839 structure. This bridge lasted another 60 years before the sheer weight of traffic, with the construction of the new Blackwall Tunnel, created the need for a new bridge, which incorporates the Bow flyover.

In 1311 a licence was granted by the Bishop of London to the inhabitants to build a chapel because they were some distance from the parish church of St Dunstan's, Stepney, and the roads in winter were often impassable because of flooding. Edward III granted for this purpose a piece of land on what was the king's highway, and the church of St Mary was built on an island site. It was a chapel of ease for the mother church of Stepney until 1719, when it was consecrated at the same time as Bow became a parish in its own right. The ancient church has undergone many changes over the centuries, but in 1941 it was severely damaged by enemy action, and the rebuilding of the tower can be clearly seen.

At the east end of the church, adjoining the narrow graveyard, stood Sir John Jolles' School and a small market place where there was a cage or lock up for law breakers, and at the west end were seven ancient tenements, which were demolished in 1826.

In 1795, Bow comprised about 465 acres, of which 218 was arable land, the rest being pasture land and marsh land, except for a few acres occupied by nursery gardens. By the 20th century Bow comprised about 750 acres, and seems to have absorbed the hamlet of Mile End Old Town, in which Tredegar Square is situated, although the residents there would probably hotly dispute this, claiming their own identity. Numerous Roman remains have been found in Old Ford, including pottery, coffins, and animal bones. Old Ford was also the site of a mansion known as King John's Palace, but very little is actually known about it. Two brick gateways, which were standing in 1764, were considered to have belonged to the palace. A 12-roomed residence, then a famous hostelry and reputed to be part of the palace, was destroyed by fire at Wick Lane in 1863.

Close to the church of St Mary is Fairfield Road, named after the Whitsuntide Fair, which was held in a field just behind the site of the former Poplar Town Hall. It originated in 1664 as a Michaelmas Fair at Mile End Green, but was later transferred to Bow, where it flourished until 1823, when increasing rowdiness and anti-social behaviour caused it to be forbidden.

Today Bow is mainly residential, and many of its elegant Georgian and Victorian houses survived the Blitz. With the Mile End Road transporting traffic through from London to Essex, and the Roman Road market a fair rival to Petticoat Lane, it is surprisingly pleasant to wander around the back streets and find oases of calm. One of Bow's great attractions is of course Victoria Park, which the council wisely made traffic-free several years ago.

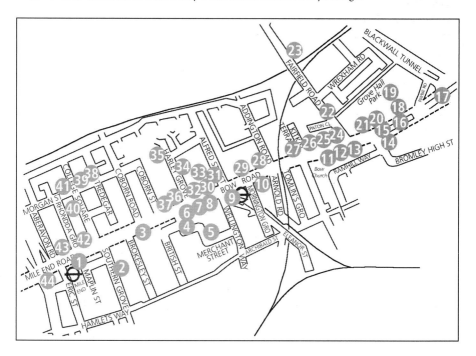

Up and Down the Bow Road

Start at Mile End underground station. Exit the station and turn right, walking eastwards up the Mile End and Bow Road, with short diversions into side streets, then back down the other side.

1. Mile End underground station opened in 1902 on the Metropolitan Line. In January 1918 several people were killed when there was a stampede during an air raid. The District Line runs through here and the Central Line from Bethnal Green to Stratford, which was under construction prior to World War Two, when work was halted, opened in December 1946.
2. Southern Grove, formerly New Grove, still has the Whitechapel Union Workhouse building, which is now part of the borough's offices.

Whitechapel Union Workhouse staff, Southern Grove.

3. St Clement's Hospital was previously the City of London Union Workhouse, designed by Richard Truss and opened in 1849 by the Board of Guardians. In 1911 the workhouse was renamed the Bow Infirmary, intended for the honest, aged poor. In 1936 the Bow Infirmary was renamed St Clement's Hospital. It was badly damaged during the Blitz, and a number of buildings including the chapel, were destroyed. Following refurbishment in 1948, it reopened, and in 1960 a psychiatric wing was added, and the hospital is now part of the Royal London Hospital Trust.
4. The Bow Road Methodist Mission, Wesleyan Hall, built to look like a Roman temple, was opened on 14 April 1865 by Revd Alexander McAulay. The building suffered bomb damage

St Clement's Hospital, formerly the City of London Workhouse.

The Convent of Marie Auxiliatrice, 26 Bow Road.

in September 1940, and was subsequently rebuilt, although the old chapel keeper's house and the 1891 Wesley Hall survive.

5. Merchant Street takes its name from the Merchant Seamen's Orphanage Asylum, which was on this site from 1783 to 1862. There is an interesting mural on the side of the mission building, executed by Ray Walker in 1978, called 'Community Fragments'.

6. No.26 Bow Road was the site of the convent of the Sisters of Marie Auxiliatrice, who ran St Mary's Home for Working Girls from 1913 to 1923. The convent was destroyed on 14 September 1940 during the Blitz.

7. No.28 Bow Road was the site of the Doric College for deaconesses training for missionary nursing as part of the Regions Beyond Missions, supported by the Shaftesbury Society and Dr Grattan Guinness. The deaconesses assisted in the work of the Baptist Church at Berger Hall Medical Mission, Empson Road, Bromley-by-Bow.

8. No.32 Bow Road (site only) was the Servants Free Registry Office and Training Home for Girls, opened in Sturge House in 1884 by Mrs Syrie Barnardo, the wife of Dr Barnardo. Here girls were taught domestic duties and found employment as housemaids. Mrs Barnardo personally supervised every aspect of their training and kept all the accounts. The office closed in 1897.

9. Bow underground station, built in 1902, is where the District Line surfaces and was part of the Whitechapel and Bow Railway, when trains were run with steam engines. The line was electrified in 1905. It retains much of its old-fashioned exterior and interior.

10. The Thames Magistrate's Court was moved from Arbour Square, Stepney to this new building in the 1980s. The original Bow Magistrate's Court was demolished and the court moved to Stratford.

● **Continue walking down the Bow Road past the Docklands Light Railway Station.**

11. The Bow Bells pub, a fine Victorian building, is said to be haunted. In 1974 the *East London Advertiser* reported that a 'phantom flusher' made trips to the ladies toilet a nightmare.

The Bow Bells pub.

Women using the toilets would be startled by a sudden flushing of the toilet by an unseen ghostly hand. A strange mist was seen rising from the floor, and when a seance was held to solve the mystery, the toilet door crashed open, shattering the glass of its windows. The pub has recently been refurbished, but retains its elegant façade.

12. The Tower Hamlets Register Offices were previously the Bromley Vestry Hall. Mary Bowry, widow of Captain Bowry of Marine Square, who died in 1715, left a bequest for almshouses to be built for 'poor men who must have been bred to be seamen and to their widows past labour'. These almshouses, eight in number, were situated on the south side of Bow Road, near to Bow Church. They were sold in 1878 to the Parish Officers, who demolished them and built the Vestry Hall.

13. Selbys, Bow Road, was the site of the former police station, erected in 1863 and used for police purposes until 1903, when it transferred to a new building at the junction of Bow Road and Addington Road. C. Selby and Son, funeral directors, were originally on the corner of Bromley High Street, at the junction with Devon's Road, before they moved to the junction of Bow Road and Bromley High Street. Their window was the target at which Sylvia Pankhurst aimed her stone in February 1913.

- **Continue walking to where Bromley High Street meets the Bow Road.**

14. The Black Swan Pub (site only) stood on the corner of Bromley High Street and Bow Road. On the night of 23 September 1916 the pub was completely destroyed by a 100kg bomb dropped by a Zeppelin in one of the first air attacks on London. The Reynolds family, who were all upstairs in bed, were found lying in the cellar. The landlord's two daughters, Cissie Reynolds, 20 and Sylvia Adams, 21, Sylvia's 13-month old baby girl, also named Sylvia, and their grandmother Mrs Potter all died. Eight-year-old George Reynolds and his brother Sydney, aged nine, along with Sylvia's husband Henry Adams, were injured. The pub was later rebuilt but the ghosts of Sylvia and Cissy were said to haunt the building. The cellar was the scene of many ghostly occurrences, such as beer taps being turned on and off in the middle of the night. The pub was demolished when Bromley High Street was widened, and a block of flats now occupies the site.

Gladstone's statue and St Mary's Church, Bow Road.

- **Cross over the road here, onto the island formed by the church.**

15. Gladstone's statue was erected in front of Bow Church in 1882 by Theodore Bryant, a great admirer of the

Liberal Prime Minister. The statue was the work of sculptor Bruce Joy. Sometime in the early 1990s the statue was splashed with red paint, in an apparent protest at the Bryant & May match factory being refurbished to contain luxury apartments. The paint was intended to recall the story of the matchgirls slashing their wrists and smearing their blood on the base of the statue, claiming that they had paid for it with their blood. However, the story itself has no basis in fact, for it was the drinking fountain, which had stood in the vicinity of the Poplar Municipal Hall, which had been paid for by the matchgirls, as the plaque imbedded in the wall indicates.

16. St Mary's Church, Bow is on the site of a chapel of ease which was built in 1311 on the king's highway. The present structure dates to 1719, when the church became a parish church in its own right. There is a 14th-century font and a Loos cross, and a fine war memorial. Dame Prisca Coborn (d.1701), who founded the Coborn School, is buried at the entrance to the church, along with her mother. The church also contains several monuments of interest, including those of Prisca Coborn and her step-daughter Alice, who died of smallpox on her wedding day, at the age of 15. The memorial has a graceful stone head, which was said to have been carved by her husband to be, Mr Wollaston. The church suffered severe damage during the Blitz and the tower was later restored.

● **Cross over again on to the north side of Bow Road. Walk up the road, where you will get a good view of the site of the original Bow Bridge.**

17. Bow Bridge crosses the River Lea and Queen Mathilda, or Maude, wife of Henry I, is credited with having had the first bridge built, after she and her retinue were almost swept away by the current as they attempted to ford the river. The bridge was arched or bow-shaped, hence the name. The bridge was rebuilt several times over the centuries, until it was removed completely during the construction of the Bow flyover and the northern approach to the Blackwall Tunnel in the 1960s.

18. 223 Bow Road was a corn chandler's shop, and one of a row of about 20 17th-century houses. The present shop front dates to the 19th century and was restored after damage during the war.

● **Return and walk through the little alley by the old convent building, and the park will come into view on the right.**

19. Grove Park, which was opened in 1909, was originally part of the grounds of

The corn chandler's shop, 223 Bow Road.

Grove Park Hall, a mansion house owned by the Byas family. Edward Byas opened a lunatic asylum here in the 19th century. The hall, demolished at the end of the 19th century, is mentioned by Charles Dickens in *Nicholas Nickleby*. In Tudor times there was a convent on this site, when the land was given to the Earl of Sheffield, Henry VIII's Lord High Admiral, who went down on the *Mary Rose*.

20. 181 Bow Road was formerly St Catherine's Convent (Alfred House), which was founded by Mother Margaret Hallahan in 1866, when the Dominican sisters came to Bow and began their work in St Agnes's School in Arrow Road. The Dominican sisters left Bow in 1923, and part of the convent was used as the parish presbytery. The rest of the building was turned into factory premises. The chapel, built in 1870, was the gift of Miss Reynolds, later Lady Hawkins. The nuns ran two schools in the neighbourhood, one of which is St Agnes's Primary School.

21. Our Lady Refuge of Sinners and St Catherine of Siena's Roman Catholic Church was originally the chapel for the convent next door. The church, in the early English style, was designed by Gilbert Blount, and built of Kentish ragstone. A high-pinnacled spire is flanked

Our Lady and St Catherine's Catholic Church, Bow Road.

by gabled and arched niches containing statues of St Dominic, St Catherine of Siena, St Rose of Lima and St Hyacinth. It became the parish church on 9 November 1870 when Bow was declared a separate parish from Stratford. The church was badly damaged in the Blitz but was restored after the war.

● **The buildings alongside the church to the corner of Fairfield Road are an interesting mix of architecture. Note the beehive logo of the Stratford Co-operative Society on one of the buildings.**

22. Fairfield Road is so named because of the annual Whitsuntide fair held in a field just behind the Poplar Civic Theatre building from the time of Charles II. By the 19th century the fair had such a bad reputation for rowdiness and drunkenness, that it was banned.

● **Continue walking down Fairfield Road, past the bus garage, until the factory gates come into view on the right.**

23. Further down Fairfield Road stands the Bryant & May match factory, scene of the successful match girls strike, led by Annie Besant, when 1,200 girls and women stopped work in July 1888. The Fairfield Works were opened in 1850 by William Bryant and Francis May. In 1971

The Bryant & May match factory, Fairfield Road, Bow.

the manufacture of woodstick matches ceased, and in 1979–80 the book match works closed and the head office was transferred to High Wycombe. The factory has since been converted into luxury apartments and forms part of the Bow Quarter complex.

● **Return to the Bow Road, and continue walking westwards.**

24. The Poplar Municipal Hall was built in 1935 to replace Poplar Town Hall, Newby Place. Note the mosaic on the porch entrance, showing the Isle of Dogs and the docks. There are also some interesting murals in the foyer of the building and it is worth going in to have a look.

25. Bow Road drinking fountain, (site only). In 1871 the government proposed a match tax of

½d on all matchboxes. Fearing the effect this would have on employment, a demonstration was held in Victoria Park and the crowd, carrying banners and flags, marched to Westminster. Bowing to public pressure, the proposal for the tax was withdrawn. To commemorate this event a public subscription was set up by Bryant & May, and a drinking fountain was built in the Bow Road from the proceeds. This was opened on 5 October 1872. This is the monument which the matchgirls referred to as having been paid for 'with their blood', for they were all docked a shilling from their wages to pay for it. The fountain was demolished in 1953, during the widening of the Bow Road.

26. The Bow and Bromley Institute and Bow Station on the North London Railway (site only) stood behind the drinking fountain. The institute was built as part of the Bow Station in 1870. The Bromley Literary Association and the Bow Working Men's Institute merged to form the Bow and Bromley Institute, and in 1897 it became a branch of East London Technical College. For over 40 years the institute played a major role in the community. It finally closed in 1911.

27. No.141 Bow Road was the home of James West, a wealthy rope manufacturer, who had premises in Wellington Way, St Pauls' Road, and Commercial Road, Stepney. One of the largest orders West received from the government was for 450 miles of telegraph cable, for submarine use. James West (d.1912) and his wife Caroline are buried in Tower Hamlets cemetery.

28. Bow Road police station was built in 1912 to replace the old building further up the road. The suffragettes were frequent visitors to the police station during the years 1912 to 1916 as they protested against the government's refusal to grant women the right to vote. To the rear of the building are the stables from where the mounted police rode out to quell the demonstrations in Victoria Park.

Bow Road Police Station.

Tredegar House, Bow Road.

29. The original Tredegar House was occupied by the Westwood family in the mid-1800s when Joseph Westwood made his fortune as a shipbuilder and iron bridge builder at Millwall. In 1893 a preliminary Training School for Nurses opened here. There is a commemorative plaque just inside the gates to Edith Cavell, who trained here from 1895 before joining the Royal London Hospital under Matron Eva Luckes. Edith Cavell later left to work in Belgium where in 1915 she was shot as a spy for assisting in the escape of British soldiers. In 1912 Tredegar House and the adjoining house were demolished and the present building was constructed as a school for nurses, opened by Queen Alexandra on 12 July 1912. The school closed in the 1970s, and the building was used for some time by the City and East London Health Authority. It has now been converted into apartments.

30. The mile post is easily overlooked, but it has stood here since 1807, and indicates that the distance from Whitechapel Church is two miles and the distance from Stratford is one and a half miles. It is a quaint and rare survival of two centuries past.

31. Note the Minnie Lansbury memorial clock over Electric House, and the plaque on the wall. The full story of the building can be found in Walk 7, the Suffragette Trail.

32. Spratts dog biscuit factory had its offices here from 1939 to 1964. Between 1964 and 1981 the building was used by Queen

Spratts van, 1953.

Mary and Westfield College, and is now Tower Hamlets' council offices. Spratts factory in Morris Road, Poplar has been converted into luxury apartments, although the name can still be seen on the building beside the Limehouse Cut.

33. Phoenix School stands on the site of the Bow Open Air School, which was set up in the grounds of Harley House for delicate children. It was believed that children with chest diseases would benefit from a programme of open air activities and classes. The school building was constructed of wood and had no heating. It was destroyed during the Blitz and the present school built on the site.

Harley College, Bow Road – note the mile post in the right foreground.

34. Harley Grove was the site of Harley House and Harley College where the Regions Beyond Missionary Union trained its missionaries for Africa and the Far East. Harley College also taught foreign languages. Deaconesses were trained as nurses for both local and missionary work. Harley Medical Hall was attached to Berger Hall, the Baptist Chapel in Empson Street.

35. Harley Grove, previously Harley Street, has an interesting building at the end, a Sikh Gurdwara, housed in a Grecian-style building, which reflects the changing East End in much the same way as the mosque in Brick Lane. Built in 1836 as a Congregational Chapel, it was converted into the Mile End and Bow District Synagogue.

36. The Lansbury family lived at 39 Bow Road from around 1920 until George's death in

The Gurdwara (Sikh temple) in Harley Grove.

1940. The house was damaged during the Blitz and later pulled down when the road was widened. (*See Walk 7*)

37. The Central Foundation School at 13 Bow Road was originally the Coborn School, founded by Prisca Coborn (or Coburne) née Forster, who inherited a fortune from her husband, Thomas Coborn, a wealthy brewer of Bow. The first school was a small building directly behind Bow Church. The present school dates to 1875. Coborn School amalgamated with the Cooper's School when the latter moved from Ratcliff. A new school was built adjacent to Holy Trinity Church off Tredegar Square, but Cooper's then moved to Leytonstone. Besides the school, Prisca also bequeathed the profits of a manor farm of 252 acres, called Covill Hall, Essex, for the relief of poor seamen's widows, preference being given to those whose husbands were in the service of the East India Company.

The Central Foundation School, formerly Coborn School for Girls.

- **Bow Road becomes Mile End Road from this point on. Walk down Coborn Road and turn into Tredegar Square, built in 1828, the grandest square in East London. It is a mixture of grand and modest houses built on land owned by Sir Charles Morgan, made Baron Tredegar in 1859. Some houses of note are:**

38. No.24 was St Philip's House, the first Catholic settlement in the East End, set up by Lady Margaret Howard, which later moved to Essex House.

39. Nos 25–26 were restored recently to their original palladian splendour. In the 1830s William Ephraim Snow, surgeon to the Spanish and Portuguese Jews Hospital, lived here for about 50 years. These and Nos 27–28

Nos 25–26 Tredegar Square, before restoration.

are the grandest houses in the square, but contrary to folklore, Sir Charles Morgan did not actually reside here.

40. No.40 was the home of Henry Wainwright, the murderer. A wealthy businessman who lived with his wife and family, Henry Wainwright owned a brush-making business in Whitechapel. He murdered his mistress Harriet Lane, and buried her under his shop floor, but was later arrested when he dug up her remains and attempted to leave the shop with them. Wainwright denied murder, but he was convicted and publicly hanged in December 1875.

41. Holy Trinity Church was constructed in 1839, built by Edmund Allgood Dickenson on land donated by Sir Charles Morgan, but the church was completed by the Metropolis Church Building Fund. The church suffered bomb damage during the Blitz and was closed in 1984. A number of sea captains are buried in the churchyard – the East London Family History Society has indexed the memorials.

● Return to Mile End Road.

42. The Territorial Army (TA) HQ on Mile End Road was the site of Deaconess House in 1879, opened by Dr and Mrs Barnardo. The TA in Tower Hamlets has its origins in the Trained Bands which existed in the East End in 1643. In 1794 the Trained Bands were reorganised as Volunteers, and each hamlet had its own company. In 1874 the various Tower Hamlets Volunteers amalgamated to form the Tower Hamlets Volunteer Brigade, and finally became the Territorial Army in 1908.

43. Onyx House, built in 1986 and designed by Piers Gough, was originally the site of Essex

Onyx House, built on the site of Essex House, Mile End Road.

House, an 18th-century house occupied for 10 years by C.R. Ashbee and the Guild of Handicrafts from 1891. The guild moved to Chipping Camden in 1903 and Essex House was leased by Lady Mary Fitzalan Howard and became a convent for the Sisters of Charity until 1929, when part of it was leased by Barclays Bank. In 1937 Essex House was demolished and the Odeon Cinema built on the site. The cinema closed in 1976, was demolished in 1985, then replaced with the present structure. The new building has gone through several names, Kentish House, Besso House and of late Onyx House. The extensive garden to the rear now contains a new development of luxury apartments.

● **Cross over the road at the junction of Mile End, Burdett Road and Grove Road. On the other side is the new Green Bridge, part of the Millennium Park. The bridge was designed by Piers Gough.**

44. Burdett Road was constructed in 1860 and was originally called Victoria Road. It was renamed in honour of Baroness Angela Burdett-Coutts, who provided the money to build the road, to provide access to Victoria Park, laid out in 1843. On the corner of this road stood La Bohème Cinema, later renamed the Vogue. The back wall of the cinema can be seen behind the hoardings that run alongside the club. It was demolished when Burdett Road was widened and aligned with Grove Road.

● **Back to Mile End underground station.**

Walk 7
Sylvia Pankhurst and the Suffragettes of East London

Sylvia Pankhurst's campaign, directed from her headquarters at No.400 Old Ford Road in Bow, was not only for women's right to vote, but for working women's rights to equality and equal opportunities. Her name will forever be associated with the militant suffragette movement, thanks to her books *The Suffragette Movement,* and *The Home Front.* But the women workers who heard and responded to Sylvia's call for action, the ropemakers, the matchmakers, waste rubber cleaners, biscuit packers, chicken pluckers and sackmakers, those who sweated and slaved in the grim factories east of Aldgate, were themselves no strangers to political strife and dissent. The success of the match girls strike of 1888, led by Annie Besant, gave hope and inspiration to thousands of women workers all over the country.

In 1906 Mrs Emmeline Pankhurst sent her daughter Sylvia to Canning Town, in East London, with Annie Kenney, the mill worker from Manchester. They found an eager, supportive band of women there. Three years earlier the Pankhursts had set up the Women's Social and Political Union to fight for women's right to vote, but very soon realized that they needed to be in London, with direct access to Parliament. Mrs Pankhurst and her daughters Christabel and Sylvia organised marches, demonstrations and rallies in London, but they could not have done so without the support of the East End's working women. Christabel Pankhurst, while acknowledging the contribution made by these women, felt increasingly unhappy with their participation, seeing them as a lost cause. Sylvia opposed her sister, and the rift between them began to widen.

In October 1912, Sylvia Pankhurst, along with Zelie Emerson, walked down the Bow Road in search of suitable premises to rent. They found an old baker's shop, 198 Bow Road, right by St Mary's Church. Sylvia painted 'Votes for Women' in large gold letters on the front, much to the astonishment of the passers-by. From here the suffragettes campaigned for George Lansbury, the women's champion, and on 10 November 1912 they organised a pre-election procession and demonstration in Victoria Park. Lansbury, the popular MP for Bow and Poplar, caused uproar in the House of Commons when in 1912 he dramatically resigned his seat in Parliament so that he could stand for re-election on the issue of women's suffrage. Lansbury was narrowly defeated, and further setbacks in their negotiations with the Government left many West London suffragette workers disenchanted, and they abandoned the East End as a lost cause, withdrawing all financial aid. The shop at 198 Bow Road, too, was closed down.

However, Sylvia Pankhurst was determined to continue her work with her 'mates' in the East End. With the help of Lady Sybil Smith, a new lease was taken on a shop and house at 321 Roman Road. For the next 18 months the suffragettes organized marches, demonstrations and processions in the East End and processions to Trafalgar Square and Westminster. On Sunday

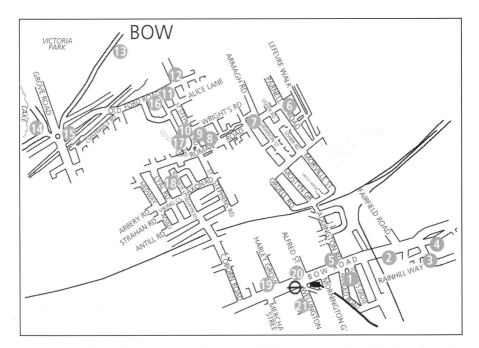

25 May 1913, the suffragettes organized a Women's May Day procession. Members from the Bow, Bromley and Poplar branches spent many weeks planning the event. The procession started at the East India Dock gates and concluded in Victoria Park. The success of this event encouraged the East End suffragettes to formally announce their own branch of the movement, at a meeting held in the home of Mrs Fischer in Old Ford Road. Groups from Bromley, Poplar, Limehouse, Hackney and Canning Town joined the Bow group and the East London Federation of the Suffragettes was formed. Soon they launched their own newspaper, the *Woman's Dreadnought.*

However, the Government's response to the suffragettes increasing militancy was to impose harsh prison sentences on them. The suffragettes in turn resorted to hunger strikes, which often brought them to the point of death. Following public concern, the Government responded with what was termed 'The Cat and Mouse Act'. Suffragettes were allowed out of prison, but were liable to rearrest should they be seen at a demonstration or public meeting.

Sylvia was determined to make her voice heard, although she risked arrest at every public appearance. However, on 24 January 1914, after a meeting with Christabel in Paris, Sylvia was told that her East London group was no longer a part of the mainstream suffragette movement.

The opening of the Women's Hall at 400 Old Ford Road in May 1914 was a significant event. It established a permanent base for the East London Federation of the Suffragettes, and for the next 10 years was Sylvia's home. The premises included a house in which Sylvia, Norah Smyth and Mr and Mrs. Payne were to live, a large hall, holding about 350 people and a smaller hall, which could hold about 50 or 60 people.

The declaration of war on 4 August 1914 forced a change of tactics amongst the mainstream suffragists. But the East London Federation felt they had to continue their fight to protect women from exploitation.

A cost-price restaurant was opened at 400 Old Ford Road on 31 August 1914 and a few months later, in October 1914, a factory was opened at 45 Norman Road (now Norman Grove), where women made toys, dolls and clothes. There was also a crèche and nursery attached to the factory.

The Mother's Arms, a mother and baby clinic and day nursery, was opened in April 1915, in a disused public house, previously known as the Gunmakers' Arms, which stood on the corner of Old Ford Road and St Stephen's Road.

By 1916 the East London Federation of the Suffragettes had changed its name to the Workers Suffrage Federation, with its stated aim of fighting for universal suffrage, with Minnie Lansbury, wife of Edgar Lansbury, elected secretary.

In February 1917, the Speakers' Conference recommended that women over 30 years of age, who were university graduates, owners of property, tenant householders or wives of the above be allowed to vote. However welcome this news was, in fact it excluded the vast majority of East End working women.

Sylvia Pankhurst's involvement with the communist movement alienated many of her supporters. In July 1917 the *Woman's Dreadnought* was renamed the *Worker's Dreadnought*. Six months later, the passing of the Representation of Peoples Bill granting limited suffrage to women saw an end to the work of the suffragettes. However, women continued with their work, but it was to take another 10 years before Parliament granted all men and women over 21 years of age the right to vote.

Although some roads have changed their names, and others have disappeared, it is still surprisingly easy to pick up the trail and follow in the footsteps of the East London suffragettes.

On the Trail of the East London Suffragettes

Our trail begins at Bow Road underground station, walking eastwards on the south side of the Bow Road toward St Mary's Church. Pass under the railway arch, and take the first turning right.

1. Tomlin's Grove was the scene of a serious incident in December 1913, when Zelie Emerson, a young American friend of Sylvia Pankhurst, led a suffragette demonstration from Bow Palace, a small hall by the church, down to Tomlin's Grove, just off the Bow Road. No.13 was the home of Councillor John Le Manquais, one of those who had voted in favour of barring the suffragettes from council property. Mounted police arrived on the scene and blocked both ends of Tomlin's Grove, while policemen on foot set about the women and children with their truncheons. Many of the women, including Zelie Emerson, received serious injuries.

● **Continue up the Bow Road.**

Bromley Public Hall, now Tower Hamlets Register Offices, Bow Road.

2. Bromley Public Hall, now Tower Hamlets Register Office, was built as the Bromley-by-Bow Vestry Hall in 1878. It is on the site of the Bowry Almshouses, built from money bequeathed by Mary Bowry, who died in 1715. The Vestry Hall became redundant when the three Metropolitan Boroughs of Poplar, Stepney and Bethnal Green were created. The suffragettes held meetings here, until Poplar council barred them from using their halls following the disturbances and increasing violence at their demonstrations. On Monday 27 July 1913, a meeting at the Bromley Public Hall was broken up by police, who attempted to arrest the suffragettes. Sylvia Pankhurst, Mrs Watkins and Mrs Ives hid in a nearby disused stable, until about four in the morning, when Willie and Edgar Lansbury came to their rescue in a wood cart. Sylvia was tied up in a sack and hidden under a pile of wood. She endured an uncomfortable journey all the way to the home of Mrs Brine, a cousin of the Lansbury's, in Woodford, Essex.

● **Turn right into Bromley High Street and walk to the turning.**

3. Bromley High Street branches off from Bow Road, and curves round toward what was once St Mary's with St Leonard's Church. Devon's Road formerly joined the High Street, and at this junction stood a horse trough and drinking fountain surmounted by an ornate gas lamp, locally referred to as the Obelisk. The Rose and Crown pub stood opposite, with the wall of the London County Council (LCC) School forming the third side of the triangle. On 17 February 1913, Sylvia stood on a cart placed by the wall of the school and made her first momentous speech in East London. It was a bitterly cold day, and her passionate appeal to the people of the East End failed to raise more than a passing interest. In a desperate attempt to create a stir, Sylvia threw a stone at the window of the undertakers, Selby and Sons, on the corner of the High Street and Bow Road. She was promptly arrested, along with Mrs Watkins,

The derelict offices of C. Selby, funeral directors, Bow Road.

Mrs Moore and Annie Lansbury. Willie Lansbury smashed a window in the Bromley Public Hall nearby, and Zelie Emerson broke a window at the Liberal Club around the corner. They were all taken to Bow police station and charged. Sylvia, Zelie and Willie were sentenced to two months hard labour, while Annie, Mrs Moore and Mrs Watkins received a month each. In Holloway, Sylvia, Zelie and Mrs Watkins began a hunger strike, which marked the beginning of a series of arrests and hunger strikes undertaken by the suffragettes in prison.

The junction of Bromley High Street and Devons Road, with the 'Obelisk', or drinking fountain, on the right.

● **Return to the Bow Road and cross over onto the central island.**

4.   198 Bow Road (site only) stood at the south side of St Mary's parish church, usually referred to as Bow Church. It was the baker's shop, where in October 1912 Sylvia Pankhurst opened the first East London branch of the Women's Social and Political Union. Sylvia painted a sign 'Votes for Women' over the front of the shop with gold paint, to the astonishment of the local people. She addressed the crowd from a wooden platform erected for the occasion by Willie Lansbury, with wood from the Lansbury wood factory in St Stephen's Road, Bow.

● **Cross over the road onto the north side of the Bow Road. Continue walking westwards, up to Addington Road.**

5.   Bow Road police station is a fine red brick building built in 1903 to replace the old police station which stood alongside the Bromley Public Hall. The suffragettes were brought here on several occasions between the years 1912 and 1916, when they were arrested for breach of the peace. The stables for the police horses are to the rear of the building, and mounted police were used on several occasions to control the women demonstrating in Victoria Park.

Bow Road Police Station.

● **Walk down Addington Road and through Tom Thumb's Arch. Turn right and continue down toward Parnell Road.**

6.   No.321 Roman Road (site only), at the junction of Parnell Road with the Roman Road, housed the office of the East London suffragettes, where Mrs Watkins, the first woman to be

This is "THE HOUSE" that man built,
And these are the Suffragettes of note
Determined to fight for their right to vote;
For they mean to be, each one an M.P.
And they'll keep their vow some fine day you'll see,
For the Suffragette is determined to get
Into "THE HOUSE" that man built.

Site of the suffragettes shop, at the corner of Parnell Road and Roman Road.

arrested with Sylvia in the East End, was installed as caretaker. Despite the disappointment of having to close the Bow Road shop, Sylvia Pankhurst, with the support of Lady Sybil Smith, leased this shop in the Roman Road. Women came along to help scrub the floors, mend the windows, and provide some basic furniture. They hung purple, white and green flags over the door and opened for business.

Roman Road, looking eastwards, c.1910.

The arch in Roman Road, looking eastwards.

7. Roman Road. The suffragettes had a stall in the Roman Road on market days, where they sold jumble to raise funds, and also the *Woman's Dreadnought*, their newspaper, brainchild of Zelie Emerson, who produced the pilot issue. The first edition appeared on 21 March 1914. Initial print runs were in the region of 10,000, but this later dropped to around 1,000. Most of the articles were written by Sylvia, although there were occasional contributions by other writers, including George Lansbury and Laurence Housman. Claude McKay, a black journalist, wrote regular articles, while Henry Nevinson also made contributions.

● **Walk down the Roman Road toward its junction with St Stephen's Road.**

8. Bow Baths, Roman Road (now demolished) stood in what is now Roman Road Market. It had an imposing façade facing Vernon Road. There were slipper baths, a swimming pool and public laundry, as well as a hall for community meetings. The suffragettes held many demonstrations at Bow Baths Hall, one of which, on 13 October 1913, was particularly violent. Risking arrest, Sylvia managed to enter the hall in disguise, but the meeting was raided by police, who set about the women with their truncheons. Mrs Mary Leigh was knocked unconscious; Mrs Ives was held up by the collar and struck with a truncheon, which broke her arm. Miss Forbes Robertson, sister of the great actor, also had her arm broken. Many other men and women were injured in the melée. Sylvia managed to escape unharmed with the help of her friends, but as Zelie Emerson was leaving the hall, a detective struck her on the side of her head. Mr Mansell-Moullin, the surgeon at the London Hospital

who examined her and found that she had a fracture of the skull, stated that if the blow had been struck an eighth of an inch further back she would have been killed.

9. Bow Baths Hall was the scene of the pageant which took place in January 1916, when Rose Pengelly danced as the 'Spirit of the Woods'. Others in the pageant were Lily Gatward as the 'Spirit of Liberty', Joan Beauchamp as the 'Spirit of Peace', Violet Lansbury as the 'Spirit of Spring' and the Cohen sisters dressed as lilies. Rose Pengelly was to have repeated her performance two days later. However on the morning of the show she had an accident at work, trapping her hand under the knife of a machine. At the London Hospital the thumb and two fingers of her right hand were amputated.

Bow Baths, Roman Road.

- **Turn right into St Stephen's Road.**

10. Lansbury's wood factory at No.103 St Stephen's Road was situated almost opposite St Paul's with St Stephen's Church. This was also the home of the Lansbury family, until they moved to the Bow Road in 1920. The timber yard belonged to Mr Brine, Bessie Lansbury's father. She joined the Women's Social and Political Union in 1906, and from then onwards, almost the entire Lansbury family were involved in suffragette activities. Willie Lansbury managed the timber yard, and was later joined by his brother Edgar. They supplied wood for the toys made at the toy factory, as well as for the furniture for the cost-price restaurant and the Mother's Arms. The yard was renamed the Russian veneer factory in around 1921, but the business later failed, and the brothers were declared bankrupt in 1926.

11. No.438 Old Ford Road, the Mother's Arms (site only) stood on the corner of St Stephen's Road and Old Ford Road. It was originally the Three Colts Arms, referred to by Sylvia as the Gunmakers' Arms. Sylvia took over the derelict pub and turned it into a nursery, a mother and baby clinic and a Montessori School. Once again, Sylvia painted the sign in gold, the letters ELFS (East London Federation of Suffragettes) surrounded by red caps of liberty. The crèche was run by Lucy Burgis, a trained nurse. Dr Alice Johnson, Dr Thackrah and Dr Barbara Tchaykovsky, a London County Council school doctor, held regular clinics there, assisted by Nurse Maud Hebbes, who was later to become the first nurse at Marie Stopes's birth control clinic. Lady Emily Lutyens, a follower of the Theosophical Movement, headed by Annie Besant, sent one of her daughters there 'to develop a social consciousness'. Muriel Matters, fresh from her studies in Barcelona under the tutelage of Maria Montessori, agreed to run a model school for young children. The Mother's Arms finally closed its doors in 1920.

12. Gunmakers' Lane is small lane providing access to Victoria Park from Old Ford Road, over the Hertford Union Canal, or Ducketts Canal, as it is more popularly referred to. It was regularly used by the children from the crèche to go to Victoria Park. It was also useful to the suffragettes as an escape route, back to the safety of their hall.

13. Victoria Park was the scene of many suffragette meetings. On Sunday 25 May 1913, a Women's May Day procession from the East India Dock gates to Victoria Park took place. Twenty platforms for speakers had been erected and members from the Bow, Bromley and Poplar branches spent many weeks planning the event. Hundreds of almond branches were carried, along with purple, white and green flags and red caps of liberty. The procession became an annual event. Hannah Mitchell and Melvina Walker regularly addressed the crowds in the park, although quite often ruffians and rowdy youths would shout obscenities at the women, or throw missiles at them. Just as often the police would use this as a pretext for breaking up the meetings.

The Victoria fountain, a gift from Angela Burdett-Coutts, Victoria Park.

- **Enter the park via Gunmakers' Lane and turn left, walking toward the main entrance. Cross over Grove Road, which cuts the park into two sections.**

14. The boat house by the lake (site only) was the scene of another serious assault on the women on 24 May 1914, when Sylvia Pankhurst was escorted to the park by a guard of 20

Llandover Lodge and the Crown Gates of Victoria Park, at the junction of Old Ford Road and Grove Road.

women, chained to her and to each other. At the entrance to the park they were ambushed by detectives dressed as costers and bundled into the boating enclosure where the policemen proceeded to smash the padlocks on their chains. In Sylvia's words: 'Any woman who attempted to hinder the work had her face pinched, her hair pulled, arms twisted and thumbs bent back.'

● Return to Old Ford Road, heading eastwards.

15. No. 304 Old Ford Road (demolished) was the home of Mrs Fischer. On 27 May 1913, three days after the hugely successful May Day procession, the suffragettes met here and inaugurated the East London Federation of the local Women's Social and Political Union. There is now a large complex of flats on this site.

● Continue walking up Old Ford Road, over Skew Bridge, when the Lord Morpeth pub will come into view.

16. The Women's Hall at 400 Old Ford Road (site only) was a large house which once housed a private school and stood adjacent to the Lord Morpeth pub. On 5 May 1914 Sylvia raised the flag of the East London Federation of the Suffragettes, with the help of the Lansbury family and an enthusiastic band of supporters. It was also Sylvia's 32nd birthday. She lived here with Norah Smyth for 10 years, until she moved to Woodford. The premises housed a women's hall and a cost-price restaurant was opened in August 1915. The restaurant was run by Mrs Ennis Richmond and her sister, Miss Morgan Brown. The two sisters were

The Lord Morpeth pub in Old Ford Road. The Women's Hall was on the right of the pub.

apparently health-food enthusiasts, and insisted on serving wholesome meals, with plenty of fibre. Some of the East End women protested at having to eat potatoes with their skins on, and large helpings of dried beans. Meals cost as little as 2d, and could be eaten in or taken away. The house later served as the People's Russian Information Bureau, and regular weekly meetings were held in the hall until 1924, which were advertised in the *Workers' Dreadnought*. The path by the side of the pub was once Ford Road, joining the Roman Road to Old Ford Road.

17. No. 28 Ford Road (demolished) was the home of Jim and Jessie Payne, where Sylvia came to recuperate after her spells in prison. Jessie Payne and her husband were bootmakers by trade, but supported Sylvia during the 12-month period from June 1913, when she was arrested and imprisoned on no fewer than 10 occasions, each time undertaking a hunger and thirst strike. When Sylvia and Norah Smyth took over 400 Old Ford Road, the Paynes moved in with them. Jessie Payne was one of the six women selected to go to Downing Street to meet the Prime Minister Herbert Asquith, on 23 June 1914. On 3 March 1914, Sylvia addressed a gathering of the People's Army, a band of men and women who volunteered to protect the suffragettes from the police, from the window of No.28 Ford Road.

- **Cross over the Roman Road; pass through the small access route, which leads into Norman Grove.**

18. No.45 Norman Grove was the site of the suffragettes' toy factory, boot factory and clothing factory, crèche and nursery. The factories were in the building behind No.45. The East London toy factory was intended to provide work at reasonable wages for women who could not otherwise leave their small children at home. They were paid a minimum of 5d an hour, and could work to hours of their own choosing. The charge for the use of the crèche was 3d, which included food. The crèche was soon oversubscribed, and many had to be turned away. Lady Sybil Smith, daughter of Lord Antrim, managed the nursery, but ill health and the demands of her family soon forced her to give up her East End activities. Sylvia's artist friends, Amy Browning, Edith Downing, Hilda Jeffries and a Miss Acheson, designed the toys and helped the women to produce them. There was an immediate demand for the toys, as

The house where Sylvia Pankhurst and Norah Smythe set up the toy factory, 45 Norman Grove.

imports from Germany had dried up as a result of World War One, but as their popularity increased, other manufacturers copied the designs and undercut the market, making it difficult for the factory to run at a profit. The first toys were simple flat wooden animals, made from wood out of the Lansbury yard. Later soft toys were produced, including dolls with porcelain faces, black cats made from guardsmen's discarded busbys, and even teddy bears. The factory was not a financial success, and Norah Smyth continued to support the work with generous contributions from her resources. The factory remained at Norman Road until 1934, when it was moved to King's Cross until 1943, when the area was bombed during the Blitz.

- **Continue walking up Norman Grove and Selwyn Road, into Coborn Road, which connects to the Bow Road, and turn left (eastwards).**

19. No.39 Bow Road (site only) was the Lansbury home where George Lansbury and his wife Elizabeth lived from about 1920. Both were ardent socialists and supporters of the women's suffrage movement. George was elected to Parliament in 1910, as MP for Poplar, but resigned his seat in November 1912 in protest at Parliament's refusal to consider admitting women onto the electoral roll. He stood for re-election on the issue of women's suffrage, but was narrowly defeated and remained out of the Commons for the next 10 years, during which time he edited the *Daily Herald*. The Lansburys were all active politically, and the daughters Daisy, Annie, Dolly and Violet and daughters-in-law Jessie and Minnie worked enthusiastically alongside Sylvia Pankhurst in Bow. Daisy married Raymond Postgate MP and was a councillor in Shoreditch, while Dolly, or Dorothy, married Ernest Thurtle, and

A plaque on the pavement in the Bow Road marks the site of George Lansbury's house, destroyed during the Blitz.

was a councillor in Hackney, delighting her father by being elected mayor. Annie kept house for George until his death in 1940, and then moved to Ilford, where she died in 1952.

20. Electric House, Bow Road has a clock mounted on the corner, a memorial to a remarkable woman. Minnie, the daughter of Isaac Glassman, a Jewish coal dealer in Chicksand Street, a turning off Brick Lane, was a school teacher until 1914, when she married Edgar Lansbury. She joined the East London suffragettes after the group had been renamed the Workers' Suffrage Federation in 1915. While Minnie shared Sylvia's socialist views, she took an active role in local politics, and was elected alderman on Poplar's first Labour council in 1919. She was also chairman of the War Pensions Committee, where she fought for the rights of widows and orphans of World War One and the war wounded. In September 1921, Minnie Lansbury was one of five women on Poplar council, who together with their male colleagues served a six-week term of imprison-ment for their refusal to levy full rates in Poplar. Sadly, the spell in prison led to her contracting a severe cold, followed by pneumonia, and she died on 1 January 1922, aged 32. Her funeral from Wellington Grove (Road) opposite was attended by thousands of mourners, who escorted the cortège to the Jewish cemetery in East Ham.

21. Wellington Grove (opposite) is adjacent to Bow Road Station. Edgar and Minnie Lansbury lived here until Minnie's death. Edgar was a Labour councillor and later mayor of Poplar in 1924–5. Lucy Cole, a suffragette, joined the household as Edgar and Minnie's housekeeper in 1917. Lucy was an ardent Labour supporter, attended rallies in Hyde Park and joined the Lansburys during their protests in the Poplar rates dispute. When the Lansburys were imprisoned, along with other Poplar councillors, for refusing to

Electric House, Bow Road, with the Minnie Lansbury memorial clock.

levy rates in Poplar, Lucy visited them every week. She nursed Minnie during her subsequent illness, and supported Edgar when Minnie died. She later worked as a cook for the London County Council and in the canteen at Thames Television. Lucy Cole died in 1993 at the age of 104.

- **The trail ends at Bow Road underground station.**

Walk 8
Whitechapel

Whitechapel takes its name from a small whitewashed chapel, dedicated to St Mary Matfelon, which was built in 1270 as a chapel of ease for St Dunstan's, the mother church on Stepney Green. St Mary Matfelon was made the parish church of Stepney Whitechapel in 1694. The church was rebuilt several times through the centuries, and demolished after being destroyed during the Blitz. A garden now marks the site.

Roque's map of 18th-century London, published in 1746, shows Whitechapel High Street as a broad highway leading out of London, with a cluster of little alleyways and streets near the City of London, which gradually get fewer and fewer until at Mile End there are only fields and market gardens, with houses lining the road on either side. Mile End Waste was a traditional mustering place for troops in Tudor times. Whitechapel stretched as far at Mile End Gate, where a tollgate stood up to 1866.

From 1708 there was a hay market along the Whitechapel High Street, where haycarts arrived from the country three times a week Originally held at Ratcliff, the Whitechapel site was probably chosen because it was the nearest spot which could conveniently be used for the purpose which was near the gates of the city (Aldgate), without actually encroaching on the city proper. The hay market was in existence until 1928, when it was abolished by an Act of Parliament. An interesting mural in tiles depicting the market can be seen at the entrance to the Whitechapel Library, next door to which is the Whitechapel Art Gallery, one of Canon Barnett's schemes to bring culture to the labouring classes.

The oldest business in London, the Whitechapel Bell Foundry, which has flourished here since the time of Elizabeth I, stands in the Whitechapel Road. It has been making bells in the East End for four centuries, and moved to the Whitechapel Road in 1738. Save for an added Georgian front the building remains almost unchanged. It traded under the name of Mears and Stainbank from 1865 to 1968 when its name was changed to the Whitechapel Bell Foundry Ltd.

Regular coaches ran from the Bull Inn in Whitechapel to Chigwell, and from the Saracen's Head in Aldgate to Wanstead and Leyton. As may be expected, there were rich pickings to be had from travellers and these coaching inns were the haunt of highwaymen, footpads and dippers.

From 1752–9 the London Hospital, which had begun its work in 1740, built its new premises in a field beside the Whitechapel Road, immediately to the east of the Whitechapel Mount.

Brady Street was the site of a ducking pond, used for the punishment of shrewish wives, and minor miscreants, while open fields stretched to the north and south. Sheep grazed on Stepney Green and Globe Fields, where cattle were also pastured on their way to the Mile End cattle market. The south side of Whitechapel High Street had several butchers' shops, where cattle were slaughtered and carcasses sold. Turkeys walked the 80 miles from Norfolk down through Whitechapel to be killed at Leadenhall Market.

Gentlemen of the city retired to Stepney to enjoy the fresh air, and some fine houses were

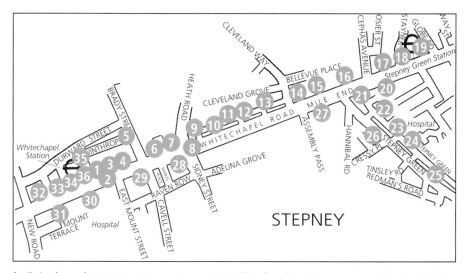

built in the early 1700s in Stepney Green. But Whitechapel and Stepney were changing fast. In the 18th century the population of London increased by nearly two thirds, due mainly to the influx of French Huguenots, Polish and German Jews, Irish Catholics and labourers from the country who came to London in search of work. Excluded from the City of London by the guilds and companies, they crowded into the districts adjoining the city.

By 1760, people in search of Sunday recreation flocked to Whitechapel to eat Stepney buns and drink ale and cider. Spring Gardens in Stepney was one of the many London pleasure haunts. In 1702 it was known as Jews' Spring Gardens and was frequented by some of the wealthy Jews who lived in Goodman's Fields.

Victorian gentlemen too, came to Whitechapel in search of entertainment and pleasure although at the end of the 19th century the self-styled murderer Jack the Ripper dominated the news. Palaces of variety, music saloons and penny gaffs, fun fairs and theatres all served to amuse the workers during their few hours of leisure. For many years melodrama was popular, and at the Pavilion Theatre at the corner of Vallance Road and Whitechapel Road, plays such as *The Bride of the Bleeding Heart*, and *The Murder of the Mount* played to packed audiences. On the other side the Wonderland offered drama, boxing, circus performances, pantomimes and exhibitions of human freaks.

Philanthropy played an important part in the life of Whitechapel during the last decades of the 19th century and into the 20th century. Canon Samuel Barnett founded the settlement, Toynbee Hall. Frederick Charrington, heir to the Charrington Brewery, began his Temperance crusade in Whitechapel, and he relentlessly pursued brothel keepers, hounding them out of business by noting their activities in his black book. William Booth founded the Salvation Army here in July 1965, preaching on Mile End Waste.

Alice Model started a Jewish day nursery for working parents in 1896, and set up a maternity home in Underwood Street, now Road, which later became the Jewish Maternity Hospital.

Maria Dickin set up her clinic for sick animals in Whitechapel in the cellar of a pub on the corner of Vallance Road and the work of the People's Dispensary for Sick Animals began on 17 November 1917.

The Blitz of World War Two caused a tremendous amount of damage to Whitechapel and Stepney, and many fine landmark buildings were destroyed, along with thousands of homes. Despite the destruction, there are places in Whitechapel and Stepney that have survived the centuries of change, and are still there to delight and amaze.

Whitechapel to Stepney Green

The walk begins at Whitechapel underground station, walking eastwards to Stepney Green underground station and returning on the south side of Mile End Road, with a detour into Stepney Green then back into Whitechapel Road.

1. Whitechapel underground station was opened in October 1884 by the Metropolitan District Railway. It was the end of the line until 1902, when the line was extended to Upminster. The East London Line to south London travels through the Thames Tunnel, the first tunnel built for transport under a major river. It was constructed by Marc Brunel and his famous son Isambard Kingdom Brunel, and took nearly 20 years to complete, opening to pedestrians in 1843.

2. Whitechapel Market was established here after the construction of this wide road. In the 1850s the traders were mostly Irish who had come over following the great famine of 1850, but by the turn of the century the traders were largely Jewish. Today most of the stallholders are Asian.

3. The Working Lads Institute was built adjacent to the station in 1885. In 1888 an extension was opened to include a swimming bath and lecture hall. Radical meetings were held in the hall in the 1890s and speakers included Prince Kropotkin and Rudolf Rocker. In 1896 the institute was bought by Thomas Jackson, and reopened as the Whitechapel Primitive Methodist Mission, which included a Home for Friendless and Orphaned Lads.

4. Lord Rodney's Head was a Victorian music hall from 1854 to 1885 and was known as the Prince's Hall of Varieties. Lord Rodney won a famous naval victory against the French in the West Indies in 1782. Charles Coborn, the music hall star, performed here for 12 shillings a night.

5. Brady Street was home to the Brady Boys Club, which was opened over 100 years ago for Jewish boys, and later girls. The clubs have now moved to north London. Whitechapel Green had a pond and ducking stool and Brady Street was originally Ducking Pond Lane. Further down is a disused Jewish Ashkenazi cemetery. Nathan Rothschild, who founded the London branch of his family bank in 1805, is buried here, as is Miriam Levey, who opened the very first soup kitchen in Whitechapel. The site was originally a brickfield which was leased for burials in 1761 for 12 guineas a year.

6. Mann Crossman and Paulin's Albion Brewery occupies the site of a brewery dating from 1808, which was taken over in 1819 by James Mann, while Robert Crossman and Thomas

Paulin joined the business in 1846. Rebuilt in 1855, the Albion brewery continued for 100 years until it was taken over by Watney's in 1959, closing in the 1990s. The brewery was the first place in Britain to produce bottled brown ale.

7. The Blind Beggar pub recalls the legend of the Blind Beggar of Bethnal Green, supposedly Simon de Montfort, but more likely a soldier wounded in the French wars, and his beautiful daughter Bessy. The Salvation Army ladies sold their *War Cry* in the pub in 1865, urging people to give up the demon drink. On 6 March 1966, Ronnie Kray shot George Cornell in the pub, in the presence of the barmaid. Although her evidence led to the conviction of Ronnie and Reggie Kray, she still refuses to reveal her identity, for fear of reprisals from members of the Kray's gang.

● **Cross over Cambridge Heath Road and continue along Mile End Road**

8. Mile End Gate, at the Mile End Turnpike, was removed in 1866 when increasing traffic made the operation of the toll unworkable. Cambridge Heath Road was originally named Dog Row. This is where Whitechapel Road becomes Mile End Road. In the middle of the road stood the Vine Tavern, demolished in 1904, which dated to the reign of James I.

9. The White Hart pub possibly commemorates Richard II's famous ride to Mile End in 1381 to meet the revolting peasants, led by Wat Tyler, Jack Straw and the charismatic priest John Ball. Seventy years later another revolt led by Jack Cade came to Mile End. The unfortunate Cade was executed and his head stuck on a pole on London Bridge. The present pub, known as Murphy's, is late Victorian and contains some fine examples of decorated glass.

10. Mile End Waste was the mustering place for troops in Tudor times. Opposite the Assembly

William Booth's statue on Mile End Waste.

Hall is a memorial to William Booth, who set up his first platform here and began the work of the Salvation Army in July 1865. In July 1888 a meeting of the match girls was held here and the Jewish tailors and tailoresses also came here to hear their leaders, including Lewis Lyons, exhort them to stand firm. In 1898 Theodore Hertzl proclaimed Zionism here and in 1917 the Jewish tailors helped to form the Jewish Legion to help liberate Palestine from the Turks.

Trinity Green, in front of the almshouses and chapel.

11. The Almshouses of the Trinity Brethren were built in 1695, possibly by Christopher Wren, though more probably by William Ogbourne, on grounds presented by Captain Mudd of Ratcliff for the use of 28 decayed masters and commanders of ships, or their widows. They were about to be demolished in the 1890s, but a campaign led by C.R. Ashbee, William Morris, Octavia Hill and Walter Besant successfully prevented this. Ashbee produced a book on Trinity Hospital, the first in the Survey of London series, and launched his crusade to preserve London's historic buildings. The chapel was badly damaged during World War Two but later restored.

12. The Great Assembly Hall was founded in 1883 by the Temperance campaigner Frederick Charrington, heir to the Charrington Brewery's wealth. Charrington carried on his good work here for 50

A section of the gate at the Trinity Almshouses.

Looking west across Mile End Waste toward Tower Hamlets Mission.

years until his death in 1936. The hall was bombed during the Blitz and later rebuilt. It is now Tower Hamlets Mission. On 1 November 1890, William Morris, Eleanor Marx-Aveling (daughter of Karl Marx), John Burns and Prince Kropotkin spoke at a meeting to protest against the Russian persecution of the Jews. Opposite on the Waste there is a life-sized bronze bust of Edward VII, unveiled on 12 October 1911.

13. The Forty Five was formerly the Three Cranes pub, the name of which was derived from the emblem of the Vintners Company, depicting cranes used to hoist barrels of wine. This was the site of the Vintners Almshouses, now demolished.

14. Wickham's department store was opened in 1850 by Thomas Wickham, a linen draper. He later acquired the adjoining properties, with the exception of Spiegelhalters. Mr Spiegelhalter had come from Germany in the 1820s to set up his jewellers and watchmakers shop in Whitechapel. In the 1880s he moved to 81 Mile End Road. The family absolutely refused to sell, so Wickham's was rebuilt in 1927 in two halves, with Spiegelhalters in the middle. Wickham's was the grandest store in the East End for 40 years until it closed in 1969.

15. The Genesis Cinema was opened in June 1999, with Barbara Windsor as the guest of honour. In the mid-19th century William Lusby developed the Old Eagle pub into Lusby's music hall. It burnt down in 1884 and the grander Paragon Theatre was built. In 1886 the 16-year-old Marie Lloyd performed here, and Charlie Chaplin made his first stage appearance here. The theatre was renamed the Mile End Empire in 1912 and in 1939 was rebuilt. It became the ABC in 1960 and the premiere of *Sparrows Can't Sing* was held here

Genesis Cinema, formerly the Empire, with Wickham's on the left.

in 1963, hosted by Ronnie and Reggie Kray with Lord Snowdon as the guest of honour. It was called the Cannon cinema when it closed in the 1980s.

16. Charrington's Anchor Brewery was built in 1757, replacing the Bethnal Green brewery of Westfield and Moss. By 1783 John Charrington and his brother Harry were the proprietors and in 1808 they stood second on the list of the leading 12 London brewers. In 1833 Charrington's

Charrington's Anchor Brewery, Whitechapel Road.

began brewing stout and porter as well as ale. At its peak it produced 20,000 barrels of beer a week. The brewery stood in what was then the pleasant hamlet of Mile End Old Town. In 1978 the brewery was renovated and enlarged, then it finally closed its doors in 1994.

17. Mile End Municipal Baths were opened on 12 May 1932 by the Mayor Cllr Miriam Moses JP. There was a first-class swimming bath for mixed bathing, first and second-class slipper baths, foam baths, and Turkish and Russian baths. The baths are now the Globe Centre for the support of people with HIV and AIDS.

18. 169 Mile End Road, the Black Boy public house (site only), was in existence for at least 100 years, until its closure in 1985. It was part of a row of wooden houses demolished in around 1900 by the Whitechapel and Bow Railway Company, when Stepney Green Station was built. It was rebuilt and after its closure in 1985 became the Fifth Avenue Social Club, now closed. Anita Dobson, who lived in Cephas Avenue, was a barmaid here before she made her name as Angie Watts in Eastenders.

19. Stepney Green underground station was opened on 23 June 1902 when the Metropolitan District Railway was extended from Whitechapel to link up with the London, Tilbury and Southend Railway at Bow. One thousand children from the area were given a grand party at the People's Palace to celebrate its opening.

20. 182 Mile End Road was Augustus Attwell's butcher's shop, one of several run by the Attwell family. Mabel Lucy Attwell was born here on 4 June 1879. She became a well-known and popular illustrator of children's books, with her distinctive style of cherubic, dimpled children.

21. Hayfield Passage and the Hayfield pub recall the time when hay carts would travel down to the hay market in Whitechapel High Street. There were once 950 pubs along the highway from Whitechapel to Bow.

- ## Walk down Hayfield Passage toward Stepney Green.

22. No.29, Roland House, was owned before World War One by Roland Phillips, who worked with boy scouts in the East End. He died at the Battle of the Somme and the house was named in his memory. There are some other interesting 17th and 18th century houses here.

23. No.37 Stepney Green, which featured in Gascoyne's map of 1703, was built in 1694 for a London merchant, Dormer Sheppard. The initials M.G. on the gates are those of Lady Mary Gayer, widow of the East India Company's governor of Bombay, who bought the house in 1714. A Jewish old people's home in the 1890s, it became the Craft Council offices in 1911. From 1916 to 1998 the house was in use as council offices.

24. The London Jewish Hospital (site only), which opened in 1919, stood next to No.37. Although mainly supported by the Jewish community, it was

A view of the doorway, No.37 Stepney Green, c.1911, when it was the Craft School.

open to all. The hospital expanded in the 1920s with the addition of a new nurses' home in Beaumont Square in 1939, but was demolished and replaced by the London Independent Hospital, which opened in 1986.

25. It is hard to believe that such a quiet thoroughfare as Stepney Green exists so close to the busy Mile End Road. The road leads to the parish church of St Dunstan, built by St Dunstan himself. Although rebuilt several times, it contains traces of its Saxon origins. Halfway up is the clock tower dedicated to Dr Stanley Bean Atkinson, which originally stood in Burdett Road and was moved here in 1934.

The clock tower on Stepney Green.

26. The Dunstan Houses were built by the East End Dwellings Company in 1899, one of the many schemes initiated by Canon Samuel Barnett. The architects were Henry Davis and Barrow Emmanuel. The flats were built to provide housing for the honest, deserving poor. Rudolph Rocker, the German anarchist, lived at No.33 until his internment in 1914. Rocker was the editor of the Yiddish newspaper *Arbeter Fraint* (workers' friend).

● **Return to Mile End Road and continue walking westwards.**

27. No.88 Mile End Road has the plaque commemorating Captain James Cook, the great explorer and adventurer, who lived in No.7 Assembly Row, behind No.88. It was placed on the only remaining wall of the original construction, demolished in 1959. This was where his wife Elizabeth lived until 1788 when she moved to Clapham.

28. The Whitechapel Mission was opened in 1971 on the site of the Congregational Brunswick Chapel, which Thomas Jackson bought in 1906 and used as his Mission Hall. Jackson, who

Houses on Stepney Green, east side, looking toward Hayfield Passage.

died in 1932, helped found the Garment Workers Union and campaigned against sweated labour. Homelessness was another social issue he tackled, and the mission still carries on his work.

29. Whitechapel post office is the terminus of the Post Office's largely unknown underground railway. Its automatic driverless trains carry up to 50,000 bags of mail a day over six miles of track to six sorting offices. Work began on the tunnel in 1913 and it was opened in 1927.

30. The Royal London Hospital originally started in 1740 in Bunhill Fields. It moved to Prescott Street, but with the need for larger premises, a site near the Mount was acquired in 1752.

Queen Alexandra on a visit to the London Hospital, Whitechapel Road.

The London Hospital was inaugurated here in 1757 with 161 beds. The Medical College was opened in 1784, the first to be formed on the model of a university faculty. There is a statue of Queen Alexandra in the nurses' garden and a plaque to Edith Cavell, who trained and worked at the London. Eva Luckes was matron from 1880 to 1919, the year she died. She transformed the nursing service and raised both standards and morale.

31. East Mount Street and Mount Terrace recall the Mount, demolished in 1830, which was 300 feet long. It was a massive artificial hill which was probably originally a Saxon defensive work. During the Civil War it was greatly enlarged as part of a system of defences for the capital. By the 18th century, trees grew on the mount and paths ran across it.

- **Cross over the road here to the station side.**

32. Fulbourne Street is named after Hugh de Fulbourne, rector of St Mary's Whitechapel 1329-36. There was a Socialist club here, which the Russian Social Democratic Labour Party used in May 1907. Delegates included Lenin, Litvinoff, Gorky, Rosa Luxemburg and Trotsky, who was introduced to another delegate, Stalin.

33. The Edward VII memorial fountain was erected in 1911 'In grateful and loyal memory of Edward VII… by the Jewish inhabitants of East London'. The memorial is often overlooked, hemmed in as it is by the many stalls of Whitechapel Market. On the sides are the figures of Liberty and Justice, with small children at their feet, one of whom is holding a motor car.

34. No.259 Whitechapel High Street was the site of the shop where, in November 1884, the surgeon Sir Frederick Treves first discovered Joseph Merrick, who was on display as 'the Elephant Man'. Treves examined him and wrote an account of his findings for the British Medical Journal. Merrick suffered from neurofibromatosis, which gave him an enormous misshapen head, and a body covered in a brown growth. In 1886 Merrick was admitted to the Royal London Hospital, where he lived in relative comfort for four years, until his death in 1890 at the age of 38.

35. Wood's Buildings led into Bucks Row, which is now Durward Street. Here on 31 August 1888 the body of Polly (Mary Ann) Nichols was found with horrific wounds. The policemen on duty called on Dr Rees Ralph Llewellyn to check the body before they removed it to the morgue. This was probably the first of the murders by the self-styled Jack the Ripper, which occupied the thoughts of all Londoners and the media for the next two months. Despite the best efforts of Scotland Yard, the murderer was never apprehended.

36. The Grave Maurice dates from 1874. Graf (Count) Maurice was the Prince of Orange and a great Dutch hero who drove the Spaniards from the Netherlands in the late 16th century. In gratitude he was offered the crown of his country, but he refused. The Kray brothers were regulars in this pub.

- **Back to Whitechapel Station.**

Walk 9
Bethnal Green

St John's Church on the Green, on the corner of Cambridge Heath Road and Roman Road (formerly Green Street), overlooks Bethnal Green Road, and it is hard to imagine that less than two centuries ago this was almost entirely farmland, so fertile that it yielded two crops a year.

The word Bethnal has been explained in a variety of ways. Lysons suggests that the name derives from the family Bathon who held land in Stepney during the reign of Edward I, and lived in a house called Bathon Hall in the 13th century. But there were many variations of the name. It possibly derived from the Anglo-Saxon 'blithe' meaning happy or pleasant, and 'hale' a nook or retreat. The name has evolved through the years and appears in various forms – Blithehale, Blythenhale, Bleten Hall Green, and Bednal Green, finally arriving at Bethnal Green. Bethnal Green's name recalls the fact that this hamlet was once a pleasant country village with its own village green, which in Charles II's time stretched from Old Ford Road to Cleveland Way.

The Roman road from London to Essex passed through Bethnal Green, and is believed to have crossed the Lea at Old Ford. Two Roman coffins were excavated from behind the Bethnal Green Police Station and two Roman coins were found in a garden in Armagh Road, a turning off Old Ford Road.

From the time of Edward the Confessor to 1550, Bishop's Hall, also known as Bonner Hall or Bishop Bonner's Palace, was the manor house for the whole of the ancient parish of Stebenheath, or Stepney, which included the hamlet of Bethnal Green. It was situated a little to the north of where the church of St James the Less now stands. The successive bishops of London were the lords of the manor and therefore Bishop's Hall was one of their residences. Many of the documents issued by the bishops of London during this period bear the name of Bethnal Green.

Bishop Bonner was ordained in 1519, and was chaplain to Cardinal Wolsey in 1529, and throughout the reigns of Edward VI and Mary he was an enthusiastic supporter of the suppression of the Protestants. When Elizabeth came to the throne the bishop was consigned to prison. After his death, it was reputed that his ghost drove a black coach around Bonner's Fields. The bishop is remembered in Bonner Road and Bonner Street. In 1550, when Bishop Ridley was appointed to the see of London, he surrendered the manor of Stepney in favour of the lands attached to the bishopric of Westminster. Bishop's Hall and its manorial rights were then granted to Thomas Wentworth by Edward VI, and remained with the Wentworth family until 1720, although long before then Bishop's Hall had been reduced to a crumbling ruin.

In 1667 Lady Philadelphia Wentworth was forced to sell off much of the estate of the manor of Stepney, and the eight house owners surrounding the green decided to buy up the land to prevent developers from building on it. They formed a trust which prevented any building on the green, which became known as Poor's Land, as any income from the green had to go to charity. However, over the years, some portions of the land were gradually built upon.

Joel Gascoyne's map of 1703 shows a pleasant village surrounded by market gardens and fields. There were cottages inhabited by silkweavers and grand houses, such as Aldgate House, Kirby's Castle and the bishop of London's manor house. Nettleswell House stood at the west corner of Victoria Park Square, and close to the south-western part of Bonner's Fields was the site of Aldgate House, a fine building constructed in 1643.

The transformation from a rural retreat to overcrowded East End dwellings began with the influx of the Huguenots from the continent. In 1331 Edward III had established looms at this hamlet with a view to fostering English weaving and preventing the Flemish from profiting by processing the English raw wool. When the Huguenot silk weavers emigrated to England in 1685, many settled in Spitalfields and Bethnal Green. By 1740 the number of inhabitants had grown to nearly 15,000 and by 1847 it had increased to 82,000. By this time Victorian philanthropists began to express grave concern at the overcrowded, unsanitary conditions in the

East End of London. In 1900 the population of Bethnal Green rose to 130,000, but the Blitz and the war years saw a dramatic decline, and after 1945 the population stood at 60,000.

The parish church of St Matthew, some distance from the green, was completed in 1746, three years after Bethnal Green became a parish in its own right, separate from Stepney. The churchyard was laid out as a public garden in 1897 and opened by the Earl of Meath. St John's Church, however, forms the focal point of the green.

There are several buildings of interest in the area this walk covers: St John's Church, the houses in Victoria Park Square, the Bethnal Green Museum, York Hall and Bethnal Green Town Hall, which was chosen as the Town Hall when the three Metropolitan Boroughs of Stepney, Bethnal Green and Poplar merged to form the London Borough of Tower Hamlets in 1965.

Walk Around the Green

The walk begins at the Roman Road exit of Bethnal Green underground station, the library side.

1. Bethnal Green underground station has a memorial plaque to the victims of the Bethnal Green tube station disaster, which occurred on 3 March 1943 and was the worst civilian disaster of World War Two. Bethnal Green station was under construction, but work stopped on 24 May 1940. In October the local council turned it into a shelter, with bunks for 5,000 people and extra space for another 5,000 if needed. There was only one entrance to the shelter with an emergency exit half a mile away in another borough. On the night of Wednesday 3 March 1943, about 10 minutes after an air raid warning, the guns from the newly-opened gun battery in Victoria Park, half a mile away, began firing. A panic-stricken crowd surged toward the station entrance. A woman holding a child stumbled and fell, precipitating a human avalanche. Within 90 seconds 173 people were dead, 62 of them children. By 9pm, 31 ambulances, six light rescue and two heavy rescue vehicles had arrived

Entrance to Bethnal Green underground station, with the memorial plaque.

and the Civil Defence began the harrowing task of clearing the scene, which took until midnight. When the casualties were later examined, the sole cause of death was found to have been suffocation, with only one broken bone. The survivors, who suffered bruising and shock, had mostly been at the bottom of the stairway, and were kept alive by air pockets.

2. The green is a triangular shaped piece of land stretching from Old Ford Road and tapering to a point at the railway line, which crosses Cambridge Heath Road. The gardens were only opened in 1895, by the LCC, as although the land was for the benefit of the poor, the public were not allowed to walk on it. The park was known locally as 'Barmy Park'.

3. Bethnal Green library, an impressive building, stands on the site of Bednal House, and incorporates a cottage and a wing of the old house, which had been used as an asylum. The library was opened in 1922 and was partly funded by the Carnegie Trust. There is a fine stained-glass memorial window on the first floor of the library, with a book of remembrance honouring the war dead.

4. Bethnal (Bednal) House or Kirby's Castle stood facing west onto the green. Erected for John Kirby in 1570 it became known as the Blind Beggar's House and Samuel Pepys recorded in his diary on 26 June 1663 that he dined at Bednal House, and heard that this had been the dwelling place of the blind beggar, although not in the big house, but in an adjoining cottage. This is the earliest reference to Bednal House and its association with the blind beggar. In 1727 it was leased by Matthew Wright, who opened a private asylum here, incorporating two other buildings, the Red House and the White House. In 1843 Kirby's house was pulled down and rebuilt and a new block was later built for male patients. In 1920 the patients were removed to Salisbury and the site was purchased by Bethnal Green Council and built on. Swinburne House stands on the site of the Red House. The new block was converted into the library. There is a war memorial outside the library.

5. St John's Church on the green occupies a prominent position, overlooking Cambridge Heath Road and Bethnal Green Road. The church was designed by Sir John Soane. It dates from 1825 and was consecrated in October 1828. Destroyed by fire in 1870, it was restored. In 1887 the church was renovated, and following World War Two damage, it was restored once again.

St John's Church, Bethnal Green, on the corner of Cambridge Heath Road and Roman Road.

- ## Continue along Cambridge Heath Road into the Museum Gardens.

6. The memorial fountain in Museum Gardens is dedicated to the memory of Alice Maud Denman and Peter Regelous, who lost their lives while attempting to save others in a fire at 423 Hackney Road on 20 April 1902. St George's fountain, a combination of stone and majolica by the sculptor J. Thomas, stood in front of the museum from June 1872, when the museum opened. It was removed in 1926, having deteriorated beyond repair.

- ## Walk through the gardens and out into Victoria Park Square.

7. Victoria Park Square at the north end of the green is associated with the Natt family. Anthony Natt acquired much of the property around this area, and he rebuilt many of the houses. Nos 16–18 were built in around 1700. They must have replaced earlier houses, as No.18 has a Tudor well in the cellar. Nos 16 and 17 were taken over in 1887 by the University House settlement. No.16 was the University Club, which shared the premises with the Repton Club, which included one of the largest boxing clubs in the country. Sir Wyndham Henry Deedes lived at Temple House, No.17, from 1923 to 1939, following a distinguished career in the army. He retired to Bethnal Green and served on the council and the LCC. From 1939 he lived at St Margaret's. No.18 houses the Institute of Community Studies.

8. Sugar Loaf Walk is a narrow turning off to the right. Although a Mr Sugar lived nearby in the 18th century, the name is more likely to derive from a public house. In 1872 there was a rope walk along the north side of the walk. There was a clothing factory here, making uniforms during World War One.

9. Montfort House was built by the East End Dwellings Company in 1901, to provide affordable housing for the working classes. The name reflects the legend of the blind beggar, who was supposedly Simon de Montfort.

10. Bethnal Green Museum of Childhood was opened on 24 June 1872, as a branch of the Victoria and Albert Museum. In 1865 the trustees of the Poor's Land were asked to sell part

The majolica fountain outside Bethnal Green Museum.

of the green for the new museum. The structure of the building originally formed part of the Great Exhibition held in Hyde Park in 1851, and was later part of the temporary wood and iron structure used to house the South Kensington Museum, now the Victoria and Albert Museum. Referred to as 'The Brompton Boilers', it is in the style of the Crystal Palace, designed by Sir Joseph Paxton. By World War Two the museum housed mainly decorative art of the 19th century and had a fine collection of Spitalfields silks, about 45 dresses, embroideries and laces. Queen Mary donated many of the Victorian dolls' houses and is said to have visited the museum so often she knew every inch of it.

11. Aldgate House (site only) dated to 1643 and the house and its gardens occupied the land where Mulberry House and the Church and Priory of the Assumption now stand at the corner of Victoria Park Square and Old Ford Road. In 1760 Ebenezer Mussell bought the most valuable part of Aldgate when the city gate was demolished, and used the bricks and stones to build an annexe to his house, which led to the house being referred to as Aldgate House. It was demolished in 1806 and replaced by houses, then in 1816 by the Park Congregational Chapel.

12. The Church of Our Lady of the Assumption stands on the corner with Old Ford Road alongside the priory. It was built in 1913 on the site of the Park Congregational Chapel, which had replaced Aldgate House. The Catholic church was a gift from Mrs Florence Cottrell-Dormer.

13. Nettleswell House, on the corner of Old Ford Road and Victoria Park Square, facing the rear of the museum, is the oldest surviving house in Bethnal Green. It became the museum

Nettleswell House, in its secluded garden, Old Ford Road.

curator's official residence, but is now in private ownership. The name Nettleswell probably derives from a 'neat's well' or cattle pond, which used to be in the front of the house at the corner of the ancient green. The house was probably rebuilt in the 18th century by Anthony Natt, on the site of a house originally built in 1553 by Sir Ralph Warren, a Mercer and Lord Mayor of London, who was Oliver Cromwell's great-grandfather.

14. St Margaret's House on the opposite side of Old Ford Road, and originally No.21 Old Ford Road, was also built by Anthony Natt. This house was used by the London Society for Promoting Christianity among Jews and was their girls' school. In 1840 it was an institution of the Guardian Society for reforming prostitutes. In 1902 it was acquired by the Oxford House Settlement and became the Ladies Settlement, St Margaret's House.

15. No.19 Old Ford Road was the home of Anthony Natt, who died here in 1756. After a succession of occupants, it was purchased by St Margaret's, and was used from 1954 as the East London Juvenile Court.

16. No.17 was first occupied by Peter Debetta in 1755, but by 1842 it was the Maritime Penitent Female Refuge. The architect Thomas Saunders restored the house in 1971.

Eighteenth-century houses in Old Ford Road.

17. St Winifred's Well, located in a six-acre field facing Aldgate House, on the approximate site of York Hall Baths, was said to have been dedicated to the saint as early as 1160, but it has now disappeared without trace. Described as a fine spring of excellent water, in 1394 it supplied water by an underground conduit to the priory and convent of the Augustinian

friars, which was situated just off what is today Old Broad Street, in the City of London. St Winifred's Well was sealed up when water from Bow was laid in Bethnal Green in around 1747.

18. York Hall, No. 7 Old Ford Road, was the site of the Bethnal Green Starch Company, which was acquired in the 1860s by J. & J. Colman of Norwich, better known for their tins of mustard. It closed in 1916, by which time the factory had taken over Nos 5–13. York Hall was opened on 5 November 1929 by the Duke and Duchess of York. It had two swimming baths, washing baths for both sexes, and laundries. The hall was licensed for music, boxing and dancing when the large swimming pool was covered over in winter and converted into a dance floor. The smaller pool remained open all year round.

19. The Eagle Slayer in the Museum Gardens is the work of John Bell (1811–1895). It was originally from the 1851 Great Exhibition, and was placed in the garden in 1927. There was also a large fountain depicting St George and the dragon from the exhibition, the largest piece of majolica work ever made. This had begun to deteriorate by the 1920s and was removed by the council in 1926.

The Eagle Slayer statue, with the Museum of Childhood in the background.

20. Mayfield House stands at the corner of Old Ford Road and Cambridge Heath Road. In 1576 John Mayfield owned the nearby field. The Cheltenham Ladies College Guild opened their Settlement here in October 1889. In 1898 the Settlement moved to Old Nichol Street and became St Hilda's East. Mayfield House became a Polish church dedicated to St Casimir and St Joseph. The church was later replaced by the Museum Cinema. In 1956 it was demolished and the present Mayfield House built.

21. Bethnal Green Town Hall, further along Cambridge Heath Road, was built in two sections, the old and the new. The old Town Hall was opened on 1 November 1910 for the new borough of Bethnal Green. Prior to this the vestrymen met in St Matthew's Church. The statue of the seated female figure and cherubs was by Henry Poole. On the Patriot Square elevation is the figure of 'Justice' with sword and scales. The new wing of the Town Hall fronting Patriot Square was opened in 1939. The interior was rather grand and ornate, and this building was chosen as the Town Hall when the three boroughs of Bethnal Green, Stepney and Poplar merged to form the London Borough of Tower Hamlets. The building was sold in 1992, and the Town Hall was moved to Mulberry Place in East India Docks.

Bethnal Green Infirmary, later hospital, Cambridge Heath Road.

22. Bethnal Green Hospital (site only), on Cambridge Heath Road, was closed and demolished in the mid-1990s. The hospital was opened on 5 March 1900 as the Bethnal Green Infirmary. The original building on this site was the Palestine Place Chapel and schools, built in 1813 for the London Society for Promoting Christianity among the Jews. The clock tower which was placed on the hospital belonged to the Palestine Place Chapel.

- **Cross over Cambridge Heath Road to the west side.**

23. Balls Brothers' Wine Merchants has made good use of the railway arches as storage. Mr H.W. Austen Balls was the proprietor of the Old George Inn, Bethnal Green. He was Master of the Bakers' Company in 1930.

24. The Bethnal Green Mission was founded in 1866 as the Annie MacPherson Home of Industry Incorporated. First set up in Commercial Street, they moved to 29 Bethnal Green Road and in 1925 to Cambridge Heath Road. The work of the mission was mainly with children in industry, especially match workers, where boys and girls made matchboxes for 2 ½d per gross. In 1870 they actively encouraged emigration and during the next 55 years the mission sent over 9,000 East End children to Canada, the boys to work as agricultural labourers and the girls to work as domestic servants. In 1925 the mission became the Bethnal Green Medical Mission. It is now the Bethnal Green Mission Church.

25. Nos 2–11 Paradise Row form an attractive group of houses on the west side of the green. The terrace was built in 1800, although some of the houses have been substantially altered. Daniel Mendoza the prize-fighter lived at No.3 Paradise Row for a time, during which he wrote *The Art of Boxing*. Mendoza was born in Aldgate and died in 1836 at Horseshoe Alley,

Petticoat Lane. He won his first fight for money in the Mile End Road at the age of 16. In 1790 he successfully defended his title of champion of England against Humphries in a fight which went 72 rounds. He was champion at least three times. Mendoza proudly billed himself as Mendoza the Jew, and it was said that attacks on Jewish people saw a marked decline during his time. Many other great boxers from the East End followed in his footsteps, but Mendoza will always be remembered as the greatest of them all.

26. No.5 Paradise Row was the home of Miss Mary Eleanor James MBE (1859–1943), known as the 'Angel of Paradise Row'. Mary James was born in London, the daughter of a Church of England clergyman. At the age of 21 she inherited a fortune of £50,000. She came to Bethnal Green to engage in social work, and use her fortune to assist the needy. She lived at

Paradise Row, Bethnal Green, home to Daniel Mendoza the boxer and Mary James, philanthropist.

No.5 Paradise Row from 1900 until her death. Mary James was elected to the Board of Guardians in 1912, the first woman to preside over a Metropolitan Poor Law body. She was a borough councillor from 1919 to 1922, representing the Progressive Party, and was then a Liberal councillor from 1928–31.

27. Hollybush Place, a small turning off Bethnal Green Road, just behind Paradise Row, gained notoriety in 1863 during an inquest into the death of a child. This determined that the cause of death was blood poisoning, from the filth and squalor of the neighbourhood in which the child lived, where cows and pigs were kept among the crowded hovels. Whole families occupied single rooms, and bandbox and lucifer-box makers, cane workers, clothespeg makers, shoemakers and tailors all toiled endlessly, earning only just enough to keep them from absolute starvation.

28. The Salmon and Ball Pub dates from around 1733. During the Cutters' Riots in 1769 silk weavers went on strike demanding higher wages and cut the silk from looms which were still in operation. On 30 September 1769, at a meeting in the Dolphin public house, an attempt

Police controlling the crowd outside the Salmon and Ball pub during a meeting of Mosley's Blackshirts, 1936.

was made to arrest the strike leaders, and three people died. Two weavers, John Doyle and John Valline, were sentenced to death. On 6 December they were hanged at the cross roads by the Salmon and Ball. This corner was also a favourite meeting place of the Socialist League during the last decade of the 19th century, and in the 1930s the Fascists under Oswald Mosley also held meetings here.

29. No.289 Cambridge Heath Road was a Meeting House, founded in 1662. In 1771 John Kello took over as pastor and it became known as Kello's Meeting House. In 1819 he opened a new congregational chapel on the corner of Birkbeck Street. Dr William H. Brotherton (1840–1882) lived in the house on this site. The house was destroyed by enemy action in 1940.

30. The Green Man Pub was listed in the directory of 1760. The court of the manor of Stepney was held here in 1821.

The Green Man pub, opposite Bethnal Green Library.

● **Continue along Cambridge Heath Road to Birkbeck Street.**

31. Birkbeck School was founded in 1849 when the chapel run by John Kello on this site was sold to William Ellis. The school is named after Dr Birkbeck, a philanthropist.

32. No.231 Cambridge Heath Road. The Backyard Comedy Club was opened in 1998 by Lee Hurst, East End comedian and TV personality.

● **Cross over to Bethnal Green Gardens and walk back to the station.**

Walk 10
The Boundary Estate, Bethnal Green

The Boundary Estate was one of the major slum clearances of the 1890s. This area, called Friars Mount, was between Virginia Road on the north, Mount Street on the east, Old Nichol Street on the south and Boundary Street on the west. Originally part of the garden of the nunnery of St John the Baptist, Holywell, the original houses were constructed in the late 18th and early 19th century, and the roads, Old Nichol Street, Half Nichol Street, Vincent Street and Mead Street, were said to have been named after Nelson's admirals. During the construction of the Boundary Estate, a well was uncovered in Old Nichol Street, thought to be the original Holywell. The following paragraphs are extracts from the *Illustrated London News* of 24 October 1863:

'This district of Friars mount which is nominally represented by Nichols street, Old Nichols street and Half Nichols street, including perhaps most obviously, the greater part of the vice and debauchery of the district, and the limits of a single article would be insufficient to give any detailed description of even a days visit. There is nothing picturesque in such misery: it is but one painful and monotonous round of vice, filth, and poverty, huddled in dark cellars ruined garrets, bare and blackened rooms, reeking with disease and death, and without the means, even if there were the inclination, for the most ordinary observations of decency or cleanliness.

'In some wretched cul de sac, partly inhabited by costers, the fetid yards are devoted to the donkeys, while fish are cured and dried in places which cannot be mentioned without loathing. Bandbox and lucifer-box makers, cane workers, clothespeg makers, shoemakers and tailors, mostly earning only just enough to keep them from absolute starvation, swarm from roof to basement; and as the owners of such house have frequently bought the leases cheaply and spend nothing for repairs, the profits to the landlords are greater in proportion than those on a middle-class dwelling.'

The Revd Osborne Jay decided to settle here when he first accepted the living in December 1886. The parish was situated on the extreme west of Bethnal Green, on the borders of Shoreditch, a small, densely-populated area which, according to Charles Booth, had the highest poverty level in East London. By 1880 the area had become one of the most notorious slums in the East End. The 5,700 inhabitants were mainly from the criminal elements, and street fights between rival gangs were a regular occurrence. In 1889 the death rate in the Boundary Street area was 40 per 1,000, twice as high as in other parts of Bethnal Green and four times that of London as a whole. One child in every four born in the area died before his first birthday.

The Old Nichol consisted of only some half-dozen streets, but it lay at the heart of the parish. Jay built a mission here in a stable, with a clubroom and a gymnasium, and a church above. He quickly recognised that traditional methods of ministry would have little effect on this community. He moved freely about the Old Nichol, and gradually his charismatic personality and unorthodox methods of dealing with his unruly parishioners began to bear fruit. Supported by a regular grant from Magdalen College Oxford, he never missed an opportunity to publicise his work and within 10 years had raised a sum of £25,000, with which he built, in the centre of Old Nichol Street, a church, social club, gymnasium and lodging house. His greatest achievement, however, was in persuading the newly-formed LCC to give the highest priority to its slum clearance schedules to the Old Nichol, or the Boundary Street Improvement Scheme as

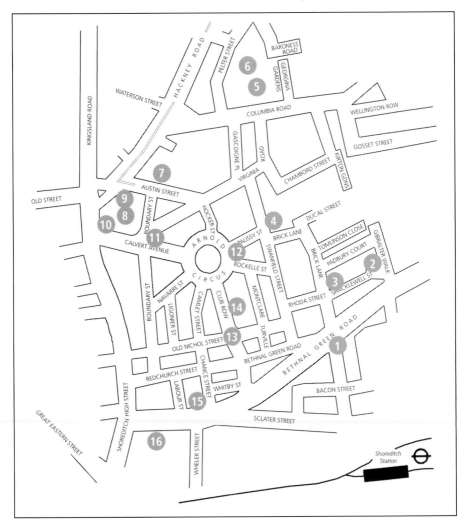

it was officially called. Following an Act of Parliament in 1890 for Housing for the Working Classes, the LCC decided to clear the area, demolishing all the houses and building blocks of flats.

When Revd Osborne Jay invited Arthur Morrison to visit the area, the slum clearance was under way, but Morrison was still able to see much of the low life of the area, and his characters in *A Child of the Jago* were drawn from those he met and interviewed. The book chronicles the life of one unfortunate boy who grows up in the Jago and the effects of the slum clearance. Morrison changed the names of the streets in his book as follows:

Old Nichol Street – Old Jago Street   Mead Street – Honey Lane
New Nichol Street – New Jago Street   Boundary Street – Edge Lane
Half Nichol Street – Half Jago Street   Cross Street – Luck Row

The following statistics from the LCC for the Boundary Street Improvement Scheme give a clear picture of the area. The streets were 20 in number and the average population per room was about 2¼, 107 rooms having five or more inhabitants each. The streets and courts were very narrow, the widest being only 28 feet across. In very many cases there was a great difference between the level of the street and that of the ground floor of the houses, the latter in some cases being 18 inches below the former. A large number of houses had no back yards and many of the small courts were of a very bad class.

There were 730 houses, of which 653 were occupied, wholly or partly, by persons of the labouring classes, and the remaining 78 houses consisted of 12 public houses and beer shops, 21 shops and factories, two registered lodging houses (153 beds) and 43 empty houses. The population, exclusive of those in lodging houses, was 5,666, consisting of 3,370 adults and 2,196 children, who occupied 2,545 rooms.

The LCC report states that a large proportion of the inhabitants of the area belonged to the criminal classes. Living in one street only there were at one time no less than 64 persons who had served varying terms of penal servitude. These statistics were collected four years before Morrison came to the Old Nichol.

By the time *A Child of the Jago* was published the Old Nichol had all but ceased to exist. In its place was rising the new-style LCC housing estate, consisting of huge blocks of flats centred on a circular park, Arnold Circus, which still stands on the spot, with streets radiating outwards. The blocks of flats were named after Thames beauty spots. The new buildings provided housing for up to 6,000 people. This praiseworthy scheme had its drawbacks, however. The new inhabitants were not the people who had been previously living there, but the 'industrious poor', and the dispossessed moved further afield into Dalston and Bethnal Green, creating yet more problem areas.

However, the novel had made such a deep impact on the social conscience, that when the Prince of Wales officially opened the estate in March 1900 he was moved to state: 'Few indeed, will forget this site who had read Mr Morrison's tale of *A Child of the Jago*, and all of us are familiar with the labours of that most excellent philanthropist, Mr Jay, in this neighbourhood.'

Bethnal Green – Shoreditch Walk

This short walk has no convenient underground station, but the No.8 bus runs along Bethnal Green Road. Start from the west end of Bethnal Green Road and walk eastwards.

1. Brick Lane market stops at Bethnal Green Road, and the north side of Brick Lane is mainly residential.
2. Gibraltar Gardens (site only) is an old burial ground beside the Congregational Chapel, just one of the many forgotten, disused burial grounds in the East End. It lay between Shacklewell Street and Princes Court and has now been completely built over. There is no indication of the site of the burial ground.
3. Shacklewell Street is a narrow cobbled street, one of the remaining original lanes. Walk down through Rhoda Street and turn right.
4. No.74 Swanfield Street is the last remaining weaver's house in this area. It was probably built during the 18th century, and when last seen was a bedding store.
5. Columbia Market, in Columbia Avenue, was demolished in 1960. This magnificent gothic structure was the gift of Baroness Angela Burdett-Coutts, the great Victorian heiress and philanthropist. The architect was Henry Derbishire and it cost £200,000 to build. It opened on 28 April 1869. The market was intended to replace the several street markets and provide a place where costers could trade under cover. However, the traders stubbornly refused to use the building, preferring their original pitches. The market was originally run by the City Corporation, but in 1874 it was returned to the baroness. It was eventually taken over by the London County Council and housed the offices of the Eastern District Depot and Housing Department. Columbia Market was used as a public shelter during World War Two, and on Sunday 8 September 1940 a 50kg bomb entered the shelter through a ventilation shaft, killing a number of shelterers. The market lay derelict for some years before being demolished.

    Baroness Angela Georgina Burdett-Coutts was first introduced to

Columbia Market, the gift of Baroness Angela Burdett-Coutts.

the East End of London by her close friend Charles Dickens. He took her to Bethnal Green, where she witnessed first-hand the appalling poverty and deprivation. She spent large sums on charitable work, and her philanthropy found favour with Queen Victoria, who made her a baroness in her own right in 1871. The baroness died in 1906, by which time her name had become firmly linked with Tower Hamlets.

6. The Columbia Buildings, in Columbia Square, were erected between 1859 and 1862 by Baroness Burdett-Coutts, who had bought up the densely-populated, typhoid-infested slum called Nova Scotia Gardens, one of the worst slum areas east of London. Surrounding the market on four sides, the Columbia Buildings were deemed model dwellings for the working classes. They were severely damaged during the Blitz, in an air raid on the night of 10 May 1941. Baroness Road, Angela Gardens and Georgina Road are all named after Angela Burdett-Coutts.

● **Continue walking toward Hackney Road, west side. This is the centre of the leather trade, where shoes, handbags and leather garments are all sold in numerous wholesalers along the road.**

Children in Coventry Ward, Mildmay Mission Hospital.

7. Mildmay Hospital. The name Mildmay originates from Mildmay Park, Newington Green, North London. The Revd William Pennefather was vicar of St Jude's, Mildmay Park, from 1864 to 1873, the year he died. He set up a number of projects and missions, which collectively became known as the Mildmay Institutions. In 1866 there was an outbreak of

cholera and the Revd James Trevitt, rector of St Philip's Bethnal Green, accepted the offer of two deaconesses to work with him. They set up their base in Cabbage Court, from where they ran a soup kitchen, factory girls sewing class and provided 80 meals a day for destitute children. In 1877 a warehouse in Turville Square was converted into a hospital. This was the first mission hospital in London.

The hospital was part of the Boundary slum clearance, and as it had already been agreed that the area was too noisy and filthy for a hospital, a space close to Shoreditch Church in Austin Street was selected for the new hospital. The new Mildmay Mission Hospital, built at a cost of £18,000, was opened in 1892. In September 1982, Tower Hamlets Health Service decided to close the hospital. It was then decided that the hospital would opt out of the NHS and revert to voluntary charitable status. Mildmay Mission Hospital was formally opened in October 1985. In January 1987, after a great deal of discussion and consultation, it was decided that Mildmay would take on the work of caring for people with AIDS. Mildmay Mission Hospital has become the model for work with AIDS patients in Europe, America and Africa. It is also the only evangelical mission hospital left in Britain.

8. St Leonard's Church, Shoreditch, is mediaeval and was originally built of chalk and rubble, later brick and stone with a tile roof. A chantry chapel was added in 1482. It has been refurbished and altered several times over the years, and was completely rebuilt in 1735. The tower held five bells, and according to the nursery rhyme, said: 'When I grow rich, say the bells of Shoreditch'. The churchyard was closed for burials in 1857. The parish stocks and whipping post survive under a rustic cover in the garden. Around the back of the church can be found the original air raid

Mildmay Mission Hospital entrance in Austin Street.

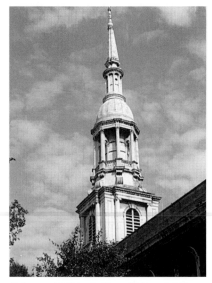

St Leonard's Church, Shoreditch, presently being refurbished.

shelter, probably one of the few still in existence.

9. The Shakespeare connection: Shakespeare probably came to Shoreditch in 1588 as an acting member of a company of players. He lived for a time in Bishopsgate, and worked at The Theatre and The Curtain Theatre in Shoreditch. The Lord Admiral's Men and the Lord Chamberlain's Men were the two main companies working at these theatres at the time, and it is certain that Shakespeare was with the latter in 1594, together with actors Richard Burbage and William Kempe. Burbage died in 1619 and was buried in Shoreditch Church with his father and brother, and many other actors were also buried there, including Richard Tarlton, Gabriel Spencer and Will Somers. There is a tablet in the church in memory of the Elizabethan actors.

The bandstand at Arnold Circus, almost lost among the trees and shrubs.

10. The Clerk's House dates from 1735. It was used to lodge the schoolmaster or parish clerk, and was used for church meetings. There was a previous house on this site which provided accommodation for a chantry priest before the Reformation. There was a corresponding house on the opposite corner of the churchyard, which was demolished and replaced with a watch house. It is now a bookshop.

● Turn into Calvert Avenue toward Arnold Circus.

11. The Boundary Estate was originally part of the garden of the nunnery of St John the Baptist, Holywell, and houses were constructed in the late 18th and early 19th century. The roads, Old Nichol Street, Half Nichol Street, Vincent Street and Mead Street were said to have been named after Nelson's admirals. This area is now the Boundary Estate, built after one of the major slum clearances of the 1890s.

The Old Nichol lies derelict, No.19 Nichol Street.

The Revd Osborne Jay decided to settle here when he first accepted the living in December 1886. The parish was situated on the extreme west of Bethnal Green, on the borders of Shoreditch. Jay built a mission here in a stable, and raised £25,000 to build further facilities in the centre of Old Nichol Street. He persuaded the LCC to give the highest priority to the Boundary Street Improvement Scheme, which meant demolishing all the houses in the area and building blocks of flats.

12. The Rochelle Street School has an interesting plaque on the side indicating the date of construction – 1899 – showing it was built as part of the reconstruction of the Boundary Street area.

The Cycle Market in Club Row, off Bethnal Green Road, c.1910.

13. Club Row intersects with Old Nichol Street, and was at one time linked with Sclater Street, from which it became isolated when Bethnal Green Road was extended in 1879. Going 'down the Row' was one way of spending a pleasant Sunday morning. Club Row was established as a Bird Fair by the 1850s, and with the neighbouring Sclater Street was also a noted market for small animals (including stolen dogs). There was a Cycle Market in Club Row in around 1910. The Row is a quiet and sedate neighbourhood today.

14. St Hilda's East Settlement: The Women's University Settlement Committee was set up in 1887. Mayfield House Women's Settlement was opened on 9 October at the corner of Cambridge Heath Road and Old Ford Road. It was founded by the Guild of the Cheltenham Ladies College, under Dorothea Beale, with the patronage of the Ladies Branch of Oxford House. In 1895 the Mayfield House Settlement moved to No.3 Old Nichol Street, Shoreditch, and became St Hilda's East. The settlement provided services such as an employment bureau, a branch of the London Marriage Guidance Council, children's care

committee work, and a children's country holiday fund. In 1944 the former Ragged School premises in Old Nichol Street were purchased and converted into a youth club. The settlement continues to provide care in the community.

15. The Bethnal Green Great Synagogue was severely damaged during a bombing raid during the night of 10 May 1941, along with much of the surrounding area.

● **Walk down Bethnal Green Road toward Bishopsgate.**

St Hilda's East community centre in Club Row.

16. Bishopsgate Goods Station was created following the opening of Liverpool Street station in November 1875, which allowed the Great Eastern Railway Company to close the Bishopsgate Terminus as a passenger station and convert it into a goods depot. The station reopened in January 1881. The new station was designed by the company's engineer Alfred A. Langley, and originally there was a plan to establish a vegetable market at the station. However, the lessee and freeholder of Spitalfields Market scuttled this plan. The main building has three lofty storeys. The first is a street-level basement, the second is the goods station, and the third is a warehouse with an iron and glass roof supported by lattice girders, resting on massive iron columns, ranging north to south. The warehouse floor is similarly supported, and the basement below the railway tracks consists of a series of tunnel-vaults, forming roadways and loading bays for the road transport lorries.

● **Buses run along here to Liverpool Street station, which is a short walk away.**

Walk 11
Spitalfields and Brick Lane

No other area of Britain has experienced the same degree of changing population as the East End of London, as successive waves of immigrants and refugees fleeing tyrannical regimes sought shelter and safety in the shadow of the Tower of London: French Huguenots, Germans, Irish, Jews, Chinese, West Indians, Indians and Bangladeshis. As each community moved into the Whitechapel, Aldgate and Spitalfields area, they built their own dwellings and places of worship, and worked at their specialist trades or eked out a living in workshops and factories. Inevitably, they moved on to the more salubrious suburbs of London, leaving behind them an enduring legacy in the form of buildings with their own unique architectural styles. One site epitomizes this pattern of change and renewal: the building on the corner of Fournier Street and Brick Lane. Built in 1743 as a French Huguenot school and chapel, by 1809 the building had been converted into a Methodist chapel, and by 1897 it was converted into the Spitalfields Great Synagogue, the Machzike Hadath. After World War Two it remained derelict for a number of years before being refurbished in 1975 and becoming a mosque, the Jamme Masjid, which serves the Muslim community in Brick Lane.

In December 1571, Queen Elizabeth commissioned a survey of the number of foreigners living in London. The population of London at the time was around 85,000. The number of foreigners in Stepney was around 1,000. The reason for such a large number in such a small area can be traced back to the City of London's practice of forbidding foreigners to ply their trade in the City. The companies and guilds held a monopoly on trades, as a result of which foreigners were forced to settle and establish themselves outside the city walls.

The communities that have had the most influence in and around the Brick Lane area are the Huguenots, Jews, Irish and Bangaldeshis. Other groups who settled in the East End were the Germans, Scandinavians, Chinese and West Indians. The German 'sugar bakers' or sugar manufacturers had originally established themselves within the City, but the noxious smells given off during the sugar refining process forced them to move further east. The tobacco trade and manufacturing industry was also dominated by the German community. The Germans settled around Cable Street and Little Alie Street, where a German Lutheran church and school was established. There was also a German Sailors' Home in Jeremiah Street, Poplar. The Baltic trade, dealing principally in timber, led to a Scandinavian presence in the East End, with the inevitable church-building – there was a Swedish Church and a Norwegian Church in Stepney, and a Danish Church in Poplar. A Scandinavian Sailors' Home was established in Limehouse, by the West India Dock Gates, and a small community settled in the area. Significant numbers of Malays, Chinese and West Indian sailors also found themselves stranded in the docks. Others just did not join their ships and sought a livelihood on the streets of the East End. They tended to remain together as a community, the Chinese settling in and around Limehouse, while the West Indians settled in smaller numbers in the Cable Street area, but there was a large

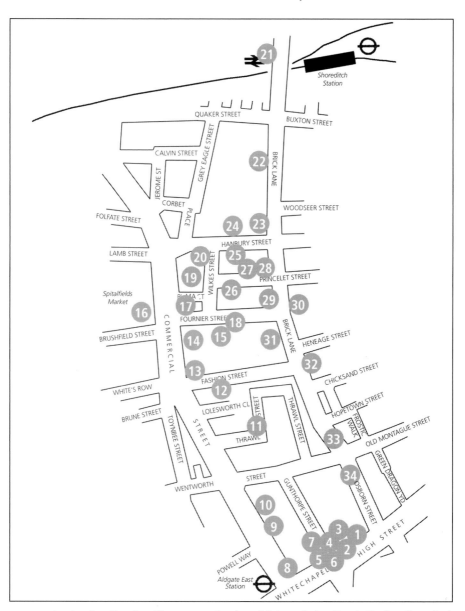

community in the Canning Town area, in the vicinity of the Royal Docks. Organised immigration from the West Indies began in 1948, as the British Government sought to replenish a depleted labour market.

When the Edict of Nantes (1595) was revoked in 1685, the French Protestants, or Huguenots, started to leave France in large numbers to escape persecution. They sought refuge in Holland,

Switzerland, Prussia and England. In the first year of the persecution some 15,000 Huguenots arrived in London alone. Among those who came to England were silk-weavers from Lyons and Tours and they settled in Spitalfields and Bethnal Green, an area with a strong and established weaving tradition.

The Irish originally came in as seasonal workers, employed at harvest time and haymaking, then stayed on in London to seek further work. They traded in second-hand garments in streets such as Rosemary Lane in Wapping, close to the Tower of London. Irish weavers were also attracted to the Spitalfields area and came into competition with the Huguenot weavers. The building of the East and West India Docks in the 1800s saw a large influx of Irishmen who came to help construct the docks and stayed on to work as dockers and stevedores.

The Jews were believed to have travelled to England following the Norman Conquest in 1066, but were expelled from the land in 1290 by Edward I and only allowed to return following a petition to Oliver Cromwell. The first group of Jews were of Spanish and Portuguese origin, the Sephardic Jews, and their first synagogue was the Bevis Marks Synagogue in Aldgate. There was already a synagogue in Duke's Place nearby. Their burial ground was at Mile End (behind the Half Moon Theatre).

The Jewish workers soon dominated the garment making industry in the East End, as well as other industries such as tobacco, leather goods, shoes and furniture. Many Jews, however, saw the East End as only a temporary home, America was the promised land. Of those who stayed, the majority eventually moved out of the East End to the more affluent areas of North London and Essex, where they have established large communities. Gradually, synagogues closed, and shops and factories were taken over by the Bangladeshi community.

The origins of the Asian community in the East End can be traced to the East India Company's working practices, namely recruiting men from the Indian sub-continent in the belief that the Indian sailor or lascar could withstand the high temperatures in the tropics, and would accept a lower wage. Once the ships reached London, the lascars were paid off and left to fend for themselves. The company cared little for their welfare, and they were often found wandering the streets or dying of cold and hunger. Malays, Chinese and West Indian sailors also found themselves stranded in the docks. Others just did not rejoin their ships and sought a livelihood on the streets of the East End. They tended to group together, and traditionally the Chinese settled in and around Limehouse, while the West Indians settled in Canning Town and Cable Street.

During the 1960s, as a direct result of the political unrest in what was then East Pakistan, immigration rapidly increased and those arriving in this country made for East London, where relatives and friends had already settled. The place they made for was the Shah Jalal Restaurant at 76 Commercial Street, owned by Ayub Ali, who in 1943 had set up the Indian Seamen's Welfare League. The new arrivals took over the premises vacated by the Jews, inhabiting the same narrow streets and taking over the same sweated industries, and even converting religious buildings for their own use. Regeneration has been slow, but in recent years, improvements in the area have been remarkable, and the area has an unmistakable Asian ambience.

This is a walk to be enjoyed, not only for the variety of historical buildings and streets to be explored, but also for the rich cultural mix to be savoured in the streets in and around Brick Lane.

Whitechapel Art Gallery.

Brick Lane and Westwards

The walk begins at Aldgate East underground station. Come out at the Art Gallery exit and turn right, heading westwards.

1. Whitechapel Library was founded by John Passmore Edwards in 1892 and designed by
    Potts, Son and Hennings. There is a plaque here to Isaac Rosenberg (1890–1918), East End
    poet and painter, who was killed in World War One. Rosenberg spent many hours reading

here. He said the books in the library inspired him to write his poetry. There is an interesting mural composed of tiles in the entrance to the library, which depicts the Whitechapel Hay Market in 178. It is believed that the mural came from the Red Lion public house across the road. Dr Jacob Bronowski, the famous mathematician and scientist, who died in America in August 1974, lived in Commercial Street on arrival from Germany as a boy of 12. He was taken to the library by another boy, and asked for a book that he could read easily, and so improve his English.

2. Whitechapel Hay Market, along Whitechapel High Street, was founded in 1708 and originally held at Ratcliff. This site was probably chosen because it was the nearest and most open spot on the great highway leading from Essex and because of its proximity to the gates of the City (Aldgate). London's thoroughfares were narrow and unsuitable for the cumbersome hay-laden wagons. However, by the turn of the 20th century this junction was also the terminus for trams and trolley buses and the congestion became intolerable. The market was abolished by an Act of Parliament in 1928.

3. Whitechapel Art Gallery was the brain-child of Canon Samuel Barnett, vicar of St Jude's Church in Commercial Street, who was keen to improve the minds of his parishioners. Barnett believed that exposing the East End common man to art and culture would inspire him to aspire to something more than the life of mere drudgery and poverty that was his lot. The building has an interesting façade, reminiscent of the Arts and Crafts movement, and it is likely that C.R. Ashbee, who founded the Guild of Handicraft and worked with Barnett, contributed to the design.

4. Angel Alley, where the Freedom Press and Anarchists Bookshop is located, is a thoroughfare so narrow that it is easily missed. There is an interesting mural on the wall in metal, which celebrates the lives of socialists and freedom fighters from all over the world. Because of the narrowness of the alley, it is very difficult to photograph the mural.

The Star of David coat of arms above shop near Angel Alley.

5. The Jewish coat of arms is an interesting sign over the front door of what was once a Jewish newspaper office by Gunthorpe Street. It is one of the few remaining signs of Jewish influence in the East End.

6. Bloom's Kosher Restaurant (site only), now a fast-food outlet, was probably the most famous Jewish restaurant in Britain, and was known throughout the world. Bloom's opened in 1920 on the corner of Brick Lane. Salt beef, gefilte fish, chicken liver and fruit cordial, cold borscht and calf's foot jelly, and the rudeness of the staff, were some of its specialities. Despite the changing population, with the influx of Bangaldeshis in the 1960s and the migration of the Jewish community to Golders Green and Gants Hill, Bloom's was the last

bastion of Jewishness in the East End. It was forced to close in February 1996, when the proprietors fell foul of Kosher laws, and a great East End tradition was lost.

7. George Yard Buildings were where, in the early hours of 6 August 1888, the body of a prostitute, Martha Turner, was found with 29 stab wounds. She could have been the Ripper's first victim.

● Walk up to the corner of the road, to Commercial Street.

8. Commercial Street was laid out in 1848, and was formerly Essex Street, Rose Lane and Red Lion Street.

9. Canon Barnett Primary School is built on the site of St Jude's Church, Commercial Street, where Canon Augustus Barnett began his work in the East End of London. In 1912 the curate of St Jude's Church, the Revd Ernest Carter and his wife Lily, sister of Mary Hughes, a social worker and Stepney councillor, decided to take a trip on the new liner the *Titanic*. Revd Carter and his wife refused to leave the sinking ship after it collided with an iceberg, and instead led the passengers in prayer and singing hymns as the ship went down. Their tragic deaths affected Mary Hughes deeply.

10. Toynbee Hall was founded at 28 Commercial Street by Canon Barnett in 1884. It was the first University Settlement in the East End of London, and indeed the first settlement house to be established in England, and was named after Arnold Toynbee, who first proposed the idea of getting undergraduates from Oxford and Cambridge to spend time imparting their learning and culture to their less fortunate fellow men. Although the hall flourished for the first 10 or 15 years, by 1900 Barnett was forced to admit that it had not brought East London into touch with its 'leaders'. Barnett died in 1913. His wife Henrietta Barnett founded the Hampstead Garden Suburb in 1908, ostensibly for the working classes, but the high rents meant only the better-off working classes could afford to live there. Clement Attlee was honoured for his work as a young man here in the settlement. He was elected MP for Limehouse in 1922 and led the Labour Party to post-war election victory. C.R. Ashbee, founder of the Survey of London and the Guild of Handicraft, founded the guild's workshop and school here in 1887, before moving to Essex House in Mile End in 1903.

11. Thrawl Street and Flower and Dean Street was originally a development by builders Messrs Flower and Dean, but it degenerated into an area which once housed some of the worst East End slums, with brothels and thieves' dens. In 1885 the slums were demolished and a new housing development for the working classes took their place. Abe Saperstein, founder of the Harlem Globetrotters, was born here in 1908 in one of the new Rothschild's Buildings. A plaque to Saperstein, placed on the building in 1963, was removed when the buildings were demolished to make way for the present development, which was built by the Toynbee Housing Association. The archway still carries the inscription 'erected by the Four Per Cent Industrial Dwellings Company Limited – 1886'.

12. The Moorish Market in Fashion Street was built by Abraham Davis in 1905, with 250 small shops. The façade has four short towers, each two storeys, with about 142 windows, and three Gothic arched windows at the Brick Lane end. Jack London lived here for six weeks in 1902, and described his experiences in *The People of the Abyss*, a book which shocked

Victorian England into action. Wolf Mankovitz, the film producer (*A Kid for Two Farthings*) was born here. Israel Zangwill, writer and poet, author of *Children of the Ghetto*, was brought up here, and he describes the street in the opening lines of his novel. Arnold Wesker, playwright, was also brought up here and his trilogy *Chicken Soup with Barley, I'm Talking about Jerusalem,* and *Roots*, reflects life in the post-war East End.

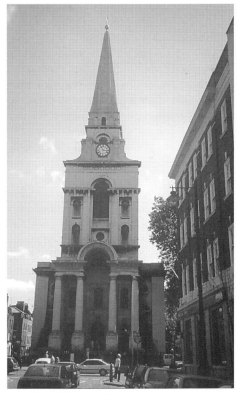

The Moorish Market in Fashion Street.

13. No.76 Commercial Street, now Dino's Grill, was once the Shah Jalal Restaurant. Ayub Ali set up the Indian Seamen's Welfare League here in 1943. He advised and helped Bengali lascars to find employment and lodgings in London, and they often settled in or near the Brick Lane area. By the 1950s there were around 300 Bengali seamen settled here permanently.

14. Christ Church in Spitalfields was designed by Nicholas Hawksmoor, and is one of his three East End churches, the other two being St George-in-the-East on the Highway and St Anne's at Limehouse. The site was purchased for £1,260 in November 1713, work commenced on the foundations in July of the following year, but building was delayed, and the church was finally consecrated in 1729. The church was constructed of Portland stone and the portico is designed on the lines of a Venetian window, which is reflected in the second stage of the tower. The impressive octagonal spire dominates

Christ Church in Spitalfields.

the area. It was radically altered during the restoration in 1822, with the removal of its windows. Further restoration took place in 1851 and 1866.

In 1836 a fire destroyed woodwork in the vestry, the bells, chimes and clock, and damaged the organ, and shortly afterwards a new set of eight bells was cast and installed by the Whitechapel Bell Foundry. In 1958 the church had to be closed because the roof was found to be unsafe, and by the mid-1970s there was great cause for concern about the safety of the structure, and there was talk of demolishing the church. However, a campaign by the Friends of Christ Church and the Spitalfields Trust eventually saw the church not only restored as a building, but returned to its full usage as a place of worship.

15. The Christ Church crypt was refurbished 1984–89 for use as a community centre, and an archaeological excavation was undertaken with great success. Discoveries were made within the lead coffins, which threw considerable light on the Huguenot community of Spitalfields. One of the finds was that of Louisa Perina Courtauld, a Huguenot and silversmith, daughter of a wealthy silk merchant, Pierre Ogier, and widow of Samuel Courtauld, a goldsmith. Louisa had eight children, but only four survived, one of them being her son George, who founded the famous Courtauld textile industry. The church-yard was known as Itchy Park, the haunt of tramps and vagrants.

Spitalfields Market in Commercial Street.

16. Spitalfields Market stands almost opposite the church. A market has been on this site for centuries, first founded by charter from Charles II in 1682. The Abbey of St Mary's Spital was founded here in 1197. The abbey was eventually destroyed by Henry VIII, following his dissolution of the monasteries. The present building was erected between 1885 and 1893, and was designed by George Sherrin for Robert Horner, the last private owner. In 1928 the building was refurbished for the City Corporation by Sidney Perks. The Spitalfields Market has been moved to Temple Mills, and the market building now hosts a rapidly expanding arts and craft market, which specialises in organic foods.

17. The Ten Bells pub on the corner of Fournier Street and Commercial Street is where Mary Kelly, the final victim of Jack the Ripper, was last seen drinking, shortly before returning home. She was later

The Ten Bells pub, at the corner of Fournier Street and Commercial Street.

found murdered in her room in Miller's Court, Dorset Street. The pub was built in the mid-19th century, and the interior has a fine 19th-century colour tiled plaque of a street scene.

18. Fournier Street was developed between 1718 and 1728 and contains the greatest number of surviving 18th-century houses. No.2 Church Street, as it was first called, was the minister's house, designed by Hawksmoor and completed in 1731. The interior of the house has a beautiful staircase. Nos 4–6 are within a double-fronted house designed by Marmaduke Smith in 1726. The street frontage has an interesting carved canopy over the doorway and is framed by Tuscan pilasters. No.10 has a rainwater head dated 1726, with the initials MS on it. No.14 has a fine Ionic doorcase and still possesses its original railings. No.27 was built in 1725 and is the largest private house remaining in Spitalfields. From 1829 to the 1940s it was the property of the London Dispensary, then it was used as a garment factory until 1977. Most of the houses retain their weaving attics, which had distinctive large windows, to allow for as much light as possible for the weavers.

A doorway in Fournier Street.

19. Puma Court is a small turning off Commercial Street. Norton Folgate almshouses were built in 1860, with wooden shutters, reminiscent of a cottage. Puma Court is the last surviving group of weavers' houses in Spitalfields. Nos 4–7 were built in 1740.

20. Wilkes Street was developed by Nathaniel Wilkes, whose brother John Wilkes spoke here to large crowds during his campaign for civil liberty. It still has many of the old Huguenot houses from the 1720s, with several interesting features.

Houses in Puma Court.

- **Walk through to Grey Eagle Street, right down Quaker Street and back into Brick Lane, then through the railway arch.**

21. The 24 Hour Beigel Shop sells beigels, a type of Jewish bun shaped like a doughnut, which used to be sold on the streets of the East End. The beigel man would take a beigel out of his basket, polish it briskly on his coat, then offer it to his prospective customer. As a result his

coat had a dark, shiny patch on one side. In America, the alternative spelling of 'bagel' is used. Nearby, also note the sign of the 'Jolly Butcher'.

- **Return up Brick Lane, through the railway arch and continue up to the brewery.**

22. Truman's Brewery was founded by Joseph Truman, a brewer in Brick Lane in 1683. This became Hanbury, Buxton and Company's Black Eagle brewery. In 1701 he started building the brewhouse and a dwelling, although the layout of the brewery could date back to 1674. The brewery buildings gradually expanded to both sides of Brick Lane, and rebuilding continued into the present century. The brewery was taken over by Grand Met in the 1980s and is now a conference centre and offices, and a

The Beigel Shop in Brick Lane.

The sign of the Jolly Butchers in Brick Lane.

restaurant and bar. Part of the brewery is on the site of a monastery and it is believed to be haunted.

● **Turn right into Hanbury Street, stopping on the corner.**

23. No.41 Hanbury Street on the corner of Hanbury Street and Brick Lane once a newsagents' shop, above which lived the Billig family. Dr Hannah Billig GM MBE was born here on 4 October 1901 to Jewish immigrant parents. Hannah Billig had a long career as a GP in Cable Street, Stepney, before retiring to Israel, where she died in 1987.

24. No.29 Hanbury Street (site only) was the lodging house where the body of Annie Chapman was found. She was the second or possibly the third victim of the Victorian serial murderer nicknamed Jack the Ripper. The entire row of houses was demolished in the 1970s to extend Truman's Brewery.

25. No.22 Hanbury Street, Christ Church Hall, also known as Hanbury College, was built in 1864. Annie Besant spoke to the women and girls on strike from the Bryant & May Match Factory in July 1888, an event which is commemorated in the roundel in the pavement. Eleanor Marx-Aveling, the daughter of Karl Marx, also addressed the Jewish Garment Makers Union here during the strike of 1889, led by Lewis Lyons.

Hanbury Street, looking eastwards, with Christ Church Hall on the right.

● **Walk to the end of Hanbury Street, turn left into Wilkes Street and left again into Princelet Street.**

26. Nos 6–10 Princelet Street were originally No.3 Princes Street, and housed the Yiddish Theatre founded by Jacob and Sarah Adler in 1886. On 18 January 1887, during an evening performance, someone shouted 'fire' and in the stampede 17 people were crushed to death. The Adlers and their troupe went to New York in March 1887, where they founded the great tradition of Yiddish theatre which had a great influence on the American theatre and the Hollywood film industry.

27. No.17 Princelet Street was the home of Mark Moses, a master tailor who employed upwards of 40 workers, and his daughter Miriam Moses OBE. Miriam Moses, born in 1886, became the first Jewish woman mayor in Britain, the first woman mayor of Stepney. She was also a founder of the Brady girls' club, and its long-serving warden. In June 1945, Miriam Moses was awarded the OBE for her work in Stepney. She died in 1965.

28. No.19 Princelet Street, now the Spitalfields Heritage Centre, was formerly the Princes Street Synagogue. Samuel Worrall, who built many of the houses in Spitalfields, built the house in

1718. In 1869 a group of Polish Jews raised enough money to transform the building into a synagogue and it is the oldest surviving Ashkenazi Synagogue in London. Some time during the early years of the 20th century the weavers' attic became the home of the eccentric Jewish recluse David Rodinsky, who looked after the building and in his spare time created a universal dictionary of many languages. His room was found only a few years ago, just as he had left it 20 years earlier. A study of his life and how he disappeared has recently been published.

29. The Jamme Masjid mosque, on the corner of Fournier Street and Brick Lane, was built as a Huguenot school and chapel in 1743, L'Eglise Neuve, with No.39 Fournier Street as the minister's house, and No.59 Brick Lane as the school. The building was leased in 1809 to the London Society for Promoting Christianity among the Jews and was called the Jews' chapel until 1819 when it became a Methodist chapel until 1897. In 1898 it was leased by the Machzike Hadath community and was called the Spitalfields Great Synagogue. No.59 Brick Lane, which was the French school and then a Sunday school, held the Talmud Torah classes. After World War Two, with the decline in the Jewish population in the area, the synagogue closed. It was re-opened in 1975 as a mosque, the Jamme Masjid.

Jamme Masjid, at the corner of Brick Lane and Fournier Street.

30. The Russian Steam Baths at 86 Brick Lane (site only), opposite the present day mosque, were run by Rabbi Benjamin Schevzik from the late 19th century. Devout Jews would visit Schevzik's baths for their ritual weekly cleansing before the Sabbath. The baths closed at the beginning of World War Two following a fire.

● **Shops and restaurants in Brick Lane are now almost exclusively Bangladeshi. Brick Lane is regarded as the curry capital of Europe.**

31. Christ Church School was built in 1874, the architects being James Tolley and Robert Dale. The plaque on the wall of the old headmaster's house commemorates the first school built on the site in 1782. The school was originally a charity school founded in 1708. In 1782 a school building was constructed on the edge of the churchyard. It was demolished in 1852,

and in 1869 a new school was built at the east end of the churchyard, the building constructed on arches to avoid disturbing the graves. It was completed in 1874. The drinking fountain is late 19th century, and has a stone basin. It also had a dolphin as a spout, but this was vandalised sometime in 1999.

32. The Naz Café was once the Mayfair cinema, built in 1935 to replace the Brick Lane Palace. In 1950 the Mayfair became the Odeon. It closed in 1967 and reopened as the Naz, the first Asian cinema, owned by Mr Muktah Ahmed. The Naz Cinema closed in 1984. The Naz Café suffered bomb damage in 1999 when a member of the British National Front planted an explosive device in Brick Lane.

33. The arch in Brick Lane was erected to inaugurate its recognition as 'Banglatown' in 1997. Brick Lane dates from at least 1550, and was a muddy lane running through brickfields, where clay was dug to make tiles and bricks. It was later laid out as a thoroughfare to connect Whitechapel to Shoreditch and Hackney.

34. Osborn Street is named after Sir George Osborn, of Chicksands, Bedfordshire, who inherited the Montague estate in Spitalfields in 1771. Osborn Street is marked on a map of 1790.

● **Turn right into Whitechapel High Street and return to the station.**

Christ Church School in Brick Lane.

Café Naz, formerly the Odeon.

Banglatown Arch in Brick Lane.

Walk 12
East of Brick Lane

Start at Aldgate East underground station, from the Whitechapel Art Gallery exit, and walk eastwards along Whitechapel High Street.

1. St Mary's Whitechapel (site only) was first built as a chapel of ease, St Mary Matefelon, in 1270. It was rebuilt several times, for the last time in 1875. It became the parish church of Stepney Whitechapel in around 1646. The church was destroyed in the Blitz and on 14 July 1945 the spire was struck by lightning, which split it in two. The ruins were cleared and the churchyard was laid out as a garden. Very few of the graves remain, but perhaps the most well-known person to be buried

St Mary's Garden, now Althab Ali Park, Whitechapel.

The vicarage of St Mary's Whitechapel, with the bell tower of St Boniface in the distance.

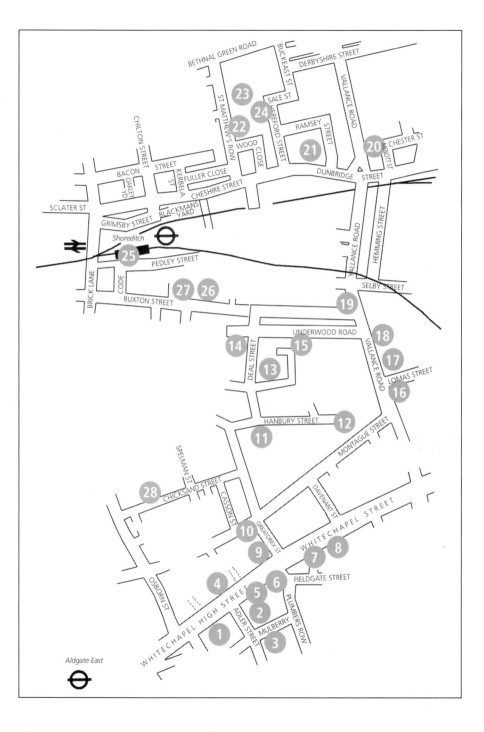

here was Richard Brandon, the supposed executioner of Charles I. Also interred here was Sir John Cass, the founder and benefactor of schools and Ralph Davenant, rector in 1669. There was a plaque in the garden here to Maria Dickin, founder of the People's Dispensary for Sick Animals in 1917 in Vallance Road, Whitechapel. The garden was renamed Althab Ali Park in memory of a young Bangladeshi man killed in a racially motivated attack in Adler Street in May 1978. There is also an interesting sculpture in the south-west corner, a memorial to the Bengali martyrs. The house adjacent to the park was the Vicarage, built in 1900 and later converted into a post office.

2. Adler Street was named in 1913 in honour of Dr Herman Adler, Chief Rabbi, who was a cousin of Jacob Adler, founder of the Yiddish Theatre. The New Yiddish Theatre Company, founded by Fanny Waxman, used Adler Hall from 1936, for its performances. In 1946 they performed *The Merchant of Venice* in Yiddish, and the cast included Philo Hauser, David and Meta Segal, Max Baum, Joseph and Ida Sherman and Julian Gold, and Anna and Meier Tzelniker.

3. St Boniface's German church, a modern post-war church, was built in 1960 on the site of the original St Boniface's German Catholic church, which dated to around 1860. The church has an interesting open bell tower. German traders in Whitechapel were mainly sugar bakers or tobacco merchants and workers. Between 1850 and 1890 there were about 27,000 Germans living in London, the majority in 'Little Germany', as the area to the south of Whitechapel became known. Although there were wealthy merchants in the community, about a third of the men were employed in the sugar refineries around Whitechapel. The work was very hot, and very dangerous. But by the end of the 19th century the industry was in decline, and many Germans left the area.

4. No.75 Whitechapel Road was Black Lion Yard, a famous East End jewellers' area. In the 1930s, of the 21 shops, 12 were jewellers. The yard took its name from the Black Lion tavern, which dated from the mid-17th century. The yard also housed a Welsh dairy, where customers lined up to buy milk fresh from the cow. Gwynth Francis-Jones wrote of her uncle, William Jones: 'Welsh people may be justly proud of the cowkeepers of Black Lion Yard... William Jones was there during the Zeppelin raids of World War One. Joshua Evans had the harder task during World War Two.' The dairy finally closed in 1949, and the jewellers followed 20 years later.

5. Boris's Photographic Studio stood next to Buck & Hickman, machine tool manufacturers. A Jewish wedding was only complete when the happy couple were photographed here. Boris moved to the West End in the late 1940s, but the distinctive façade of his studio, with its art deco addition to the Victorian building, makes it easily recognisable.

6. The Whitechapel Bell Foundry, one of the most famous bell foundries in the world, and probably the longest established, was founded by Robert Mot in Essex Street in 1570. It moved to its present site in the Whitechapel Road in 1738 in what was the Artichoke coaching inn. Save for an added Georgian front the building remains almost unchanged. The original harness room and stables existed until 1969, and there was also a lead water tank dated 1650. The bell foundry traded under the name of Mears and Stainbank from 1865 to 1968, when its name was changed to the Whitechapel Bell Foundry Ltd.

Through the centuries bells for famous churches all over Britain have been cast here.

The Whitechapel Bell Foundry.

The Whitechapel Bell Foundry courtyard.

Between 1570 and 1650 this was the only important London foundry and after the Great Fire of London, as churches were rebuilt all over the City, Whitechapel supplied the bells for many fine Wren churches. The original American Liberty Bell was cast here in 1752. It cracked soon after it was hung but was recast in Philadelphia, using the same cast and lettering. Big Ben was cast here in 1858 after the original bell made at Stockton-on-Tees had cracked during testing at Palace Yard.

7. The East London Mosque was built in 1985, with a large donation of one million pounds from the government of Saudi Arabia. It is the place of worship for many East End Bangladeshis, and the striking building has become a landmark in the Whitechapel Road.

8. The Citröen showroom and garage is on the site of the Rivoli Cinema, which opened in 1923 and was destroyed by enemy action during World War Two. St Mary's Whitechapel underground station stood next door to it. The site is now covered by the car showroom and garage.

The East London Mosque in Whitechapel Road.

● **Turn left into Greatorex Street.**

9. Greatorex Street is named after Daniel Greatorex, the sailor's chaplain, who worked for many years at St Paul's Church in Dock Street, formerly known as Great Garden Street. The Great Garden Street Synagogue in Morris Lederman House has been closed since 1995, and was one of the last Jewish places of worship in the area.

10. The Kosher Luncheon Club has now closed. The Luncheon Club was a favourite place for elderly East End Jewish men and women to have a cheap and nourishing midday meal, and non-Jewish Eastenders also took advantage of the excellent meals served there.

● **Turn right down Hanbury Street East (formerly Kingward Street).**

11. Kingward Street was originally King Edward Street and the site of King Edward Ragged School, which was one of the largest in the area. The 'Church for the Ragged Poor' was a chapel built for the poor.

12. The Brady centre girls' club in Hanbury Street East was set up by Miriam Moses for Jewish girls who previously used part of the Brady boys' club.

13. The Victoria Cottages in Deal Street were built in 1865, as the final part of the scheme implemented by the Metropolitan Association for Improving the Dwellings of the Industrious Classes. This housing scheme was criticized at the time, as the cottages were considered to be more suitable for the suburbs, and it was thought that the land could have been used to house more people.

14. St Anne's Catholic church, designed by Gilbert Blount, was built in 1855 with strong Pugin influences, for the large Irish population which had settled in the Brick Lane area. The French Marist Fathers came here first, set up St Patrick's Boys' School and a small chapel, and later built the church.

15. The Jewish Maternity Hospital in Underwood Road was founded by Alice Model. She began her work in the East End in the 1890s, first by sending nurses to help the sick at home, then by founding a Jewish day nursery for the children of working mothers. The hospital later

The entrance to St Anne's Catholic Church in Underwood Road.

The Jewish Maternity Hospital building, now used by the council.

Bengali posters in Vallance Road.

The top of the drinking fountain points to the site of the first clinic opened by the PDSA, with Lister House on the right, the site of St Peter's Hospital, Vallance Road.

moved to Stoke Newington and is now known as the Bearsted Memorial Hospital. The building is now used as council offices.

● Walk down Underwood Road to Vallence Road.

16. The People's Dispensary for Sick Animals (PDSA) was founded here in Vallance Road by Maria Dickin, on 17 November 1917. She had come to the East End hoping to engage in social work, but the sight of injured donkeys, cats and dogs roaming the streets appalled her, and she decided that helping animals was to be her mission. The work began in the cellar of a pub on the corner of Vallance Road and Fulbourne Street. At No.72 Vallance Road was the Grasshopper pub, which in 1911 was run by Mrs Elizabeth Lazenby and in 1919 by Henry Cohen. Within two months the PDSA had moved its premises to 7 Harford Street, Mile End, opposite the People's Palace, today the Queen Mary and Westfield College, but within four years the PDSA moved its head dispensary to 542 Commercial Road, where they remained right up to the 1950s.

17. The Whitechapel Union Workhouse (site only) was later an infirmary which became in 1924 St Peter's Hospital, a branch of the Royal London Hospital. During World War One the matron was Mary Mowatt, remembered for her bravery in reassuring her patients during the Zeppelin raids. It was destroyed during World War Two. Lister House has been built on the approximate site of the workhouse.

18. Hughes Mansions, named after Thomas Hughes, author of *Tom Brown's Schooldays*, were the scene of the last V2 rocket attack of World War Two, when on 27 March 1945 at 7.25am a rocket hit the middle block of flats, wrecking 60 of the 94 flats. The final toll was 134 dead and 48 injured, and most of the casualties were from Jewish families. In some instances, the entire family perished.

19. No.71 Vallance Road, the Dew Drop Inn, was the home of Mary Hughes, Stepney councillor and daughter of Thomas Hughes. She came to the East End in 1897 to live with her sister Lily and brother-in-law Ernest Carter, curate at St Jude's Whitechapel. Her relatives perished on the *Titanic*. Mary, a compassionate woman, kept an open house, and made everyone welcome, with a cup of tea and a bed for the night. She lived here at the corner of Buxton Street from 1926 to 1941.

The Dew Drop Inn, the home of Mary Hughes, with commemorative plaque.

20. No.178 Vallance Road (demolished) was the home of the Kray family. The twins Ronnie and Reggie Kray, and their brother Charlie, lived here with their mother Violet. They embarked on a life of crime, which was to have a significant effect on the lives of many Eastenders.

- **Turn left into Dunbridge Street.**

21. The Bethnal Green Baths (site only) in Cheshire Street, with signs for men's and women's separate entrances, were being demolished when last seen. Part of the derelict building was used by the Repton boys' club.

- **Turn right into Wood Close.**

22. The watch house in the south-west corner of St Matthew's churchyard is where a watchman, armed with a rattle and a blunderbuss, stood guard over the graves, for body-snatchers were at work doing a brisk trade providing corpses for the medical schools. The Anatomy Act of 1832 finally put an end to this trade.
23. St Matthew's parish church, built in 1756, was considerably damaged by enemy action in

St Matthew's parish church, Bethnal Green, with its original spire, before the damage sustained during the Blitz.

World War Two, and has since been rebuilt. In 1743 Bethnal Green became a parish in its own right by an Act of Parliament. The need for a church in Bethnal Green had been recognised as early as 1711, when the decision was taken to build 50 new churches in London, and eventually St Matthew's Church was built between 1743 and 1746. The architect was George Dance, who had also designed the Mansion House. Ebeneezer Mussell, who was a trustee and a vestryman, laid the foundation stone and presented a fine silver chalice. Mr Mussell lived at what was later known as Aldgate House, which stood in Victoria Park Square. Another treasure offered to the church was the silver-headed Parish Beadle's mace (dated 1690), engraved with the figure of the blind beggar and inscribed with the names of the parish officials. The church was destroyed by a fire on Sunday 18 December 1859, but was rebuilt and reopened two years later. Seventy-nine years later, on the night of 7 September 1940, incendiary bombs fell on the church and by the morning only the outer walls and the tall clock tower were standing. On Saturday 28 June 1952 a temporary church was opened within the ruined walls, until finally the church was fully restored and reopened on 15 July 1961, at a cost of £60,000. The great and controversial curate of St Matthew's Church was the Revd Stewart Headlam, who founded the Guild of St Matthew.

24. The churchyard was converted into a public garden by the Metropolitan Public Gardens Association in 1897. Dog-fighting and bullock hunting were regular events held in the streets, and every Sunday morning hundreds would gather in a field adjoining St Matthew's churchyard where these sports took place. One Sunday morning, a bullock was hunted in the churchyard to the great consternation of the congregation.

St Patrick's School, Buxton Street.

- **Walk down St Matthew's Row into Cheshire Street, a traditional Sunday street market area, which was a well known bird and animal market. Walk over the footbridge which crosses the railway line (not for the fainthearted) and turn right toward the station. Or, walk up to the junction with Brick Lane, turn left and then left again into Pedley Street.**

25. Shoreditch underground station, almost lost in the back streets of Brick Lane, has a limited service for both British Rail and the underground.
26. St Patrick's School, Buxton Street, was built in 1848 and first used as a boys' school and chapel. It was opened by Father Quiblier for Irish Catholics. He invited the Marist Fathers to take over the mission. They taught the boys and a girls' school was opened in Underwood Road, where they were taught by Mrs Mary McCarthy. In 1857 a site was acquired in Hunton (Hunt) Court and the Marist Sisters came over from France to teach the girls. The building has been refurbished into private flats.
27. The vicarage and church hall of All Saints" Church stood next door to the St Patrick's School building. The church was built in 1839 and demolished in 1951. The site of the church was formerly part of the workhouse of Mile End New Town. The workhouse was opened in 1783 and closed after the passing of the Poor Law Amendment Act in 1834. All Saints" Church was built in the Norman style, by architect Thomas Larkins Walker, a pupil of Pugin. There was also a school founded by the Quakers here in 1812.

- **Walk up Spital Street and into Spelman Street.**

28. Chicksand Street (site only) was the location of Isaac Glassman's coal depot. Glassman was the father of Minnie Lansbury and together with Minnie's husband, Edgar Lansbury, the son of George Lansbury, was involved in the sale of the Russian Crown Jewels, seized during the Russian Revolution in 1916. He helped to hide them in the coal shed, while their sale was being negotiated. The money from the sale was offered to George Lansbury to help support his paper the *Daily Herald*, but he refused to have anything to do with it. Although questions were asked in Parliament about this affair, it is not clear exactly what happened to the money, although it is now known that the jewels found their way to an American museum.

- **Walk up Osborn Street and back to Aldgate East station.**